Dena Michelli is an executive coach and leadership development specialist who works across cultures in business school and organizational settings. She is particularly interested in how people move through transition and change and undertook research to map this process for her PhD.

Assertiveness In A Week

Dena Michelli

First published in Great Britain in 1994 by Hodder & Stoughton. An Hachette UK company.

This revised, updated edition published in 2016 by John Murray Learning

British Library Cataloguing in Publication Data: a catalogue record for this title is available from the British Library.

Library of Congress Catalog Card Number: on file.

Paperback ISBN 978 1 473 62283 8

Ebook ISBN 978 1 444 15873 1

1

Typeset by Cenveo® Publisher Services.

Printed and bound in Great Britain by CPI Group (UK) Ltd., Croydon, CR0 4YY

John Murray Learning policy is to use papers that are natural, renewable and recyclable products and made from wood grown in sustainable forests. The logging and manufacturing processes are expected to conform to the environmental regulations of the country of origin.

John Murray Learning
Carmelite House
50 Victoria Embankment
London EC4Y 0DZ
www.hodder.co.uk

Also available in ebook

Contents

Introduction

Much has been spoken about the assertive communication style, not all of it complimentary! Many people confuse it with being aggressive, bamboozling others into submission and getting what *you* want, despite what *they* want. However, assertive communication is not domineering; it's just a means of saying what you mean, meaning what you say and allowing others to do the same.

Taking the decision to adopt *assertive* behaviour will mark the beginning of a new way of life: a way of life where you make your own decisions and choices without feeling guilty, and where *you* are in control, not those around you.

By working through some simple steps, and by testing the techniques out in a 'safe' environment, you will soon become confident in your new-found powers of assertion. You will be able to command the respect of others, achieve your personal and professional goals and raise your self-esteem.

The steps to assertive behaviour are:

● Understand the different styles of communication and the effect they have.
● Identify your own style(s) of communication.
● Know your own worth *and* the worth of others.
● Be clear about your goals.
● Be prepared to learn from your successes *and* failures.
● Be flexible, and don't expect too much.
● Learn to listen.

Dena Michelli

SUNDAY

Preparing the foundations

Today we will prepare the foundations for developing assertive behaviour and learn the different styles of communication: passive, passive/aggressive, aggressive and assertive.

This is the beginning of a long journey but it will be one that you'll not regret as it puts you in the driving seat of your own life. This is the point – it is you who drives your life, not others, nor circumstances. You may make mistakes from time to time but, as your assertiveness skills advance, you'll develop the understanding and the resources to pick yourself up, brush yourself down, and start all over again!

There are two main tasks here. The first is to identify your own style of communication:

- passive
- passive/aggressive
- aggressive
- assertive.

Your second task is to know your worth:

- understand yourself
- accept yourself for the way you are
- decide to change – *if you want to*
- give yourself permission to succeed – *and fail*.

Communication styles

In order to understand ourselves, and why we don't behave assertively, we must first examine our current **pattern of behaviour**. We will not dwell on our failures; we will merely use them for information – and for our motivation to change.

Note your behavioural pattern in both your personal and professional life. It is these behaviours that determine the way people respond to you and it is these behaviours that determine the outcome of all your communication.

If you have difficulty identifying these patterns in yourself, ask a friend to help – but remember, they are doing you a favour so try not to get defensive.

For instance: are you very aggressive, uncompromising, fixed in your views, intolerant or impatient? Are you sarcastic, manipulative, dismissive, arrogant or superior? Are you acquiescent, apologetic, deferring, self-effacing or inferior?

It is interesting to note that most people who want to develop assertive behaviour fit into the last category – that of 'victim'.

What's your message?

People always treat you the way you 'ask' to be treated. Understanding what you are 'asking for' is half the battle. You may think you are using assertive language but the way in which you convey your message and the demeanour you adopt when you do so can counteract any intention to be assertive and can undermine your success in doing so. Try 'sitting on your own shoulder' and observing yourself in action. What are you doing? What are people's reactions to you? Are you getting your message across unambiguously? By observing yourself carefully, and honestly, you can identify the changes you'd like to make and make the changes that *will* make a difference.

Try not to feel hopeless at this point: from now on, everything is a positive step.

TIP   *Remember, all it takes to change is a decision*.

Most people's behaviour patterns will demonstrate some characteristics from each of the four categories noted above – **passive, passive/aggressive, aggressive** and **assertive** – depending on the circumstances of the communication. However, one category will most likely dominate your style. Read through the descriptions below and see which one holds true for you most of the time.

Passive

Passive behaviour is usually associated with the 'loser': one who is always backing down, giving in and being submissive. Apologies are rife in this mode of communication, as are reluctant agreements and negative statements about oneself. Passive behaviour conveys the message 'You're OK, I'm not OK.'

Passive/aggressive

Passive/aggressive behaviour is usually associated with the 'saboteur'. It is by no means overt, but the aggressive motivation is obvious nonetheless. The distinguishing features of this mode of communication are sarcastic comments, comments with double meanings and non-verbal signals such as mockingly gazing heavenwards. The underlying message is 'I'm not OK, you're not OK.'

Aggressive

Aggressive behaviour takes no account of the rights of others. Although this person may be perceived to be a 'go-getter' or one of life's 'winners', they are usually feared and their style encourages deceitful behaviour from others who would rather not face up to their wrath. The message conveyed by this person is 'I'm OK, you're not OK.'

Assertive

Assertive communication does not diminish or 'put down' another human being, it does not trespass on any human rights and it does not shy away from important issues. Rather, it encourages satisfactory communication where everyone's needs are met in the best way. The identifying characteristic of assertive behaviour is the use of 'I' statements. This indicates that the person communicating is taking responsibility for the message that is being conveyed. For example, 'I am not happy with this decision, I would like to discuss it further.' This form of communication is based on respect for oneself and others. It is driven by the belief that 'I'm OK, you're OK.' There are no losers.

A word of caution. Assertive behaviour does not necessarily mean that you get your way all the time. It does mean that the chances of getting to the best solution, with everyone's self-esteem intact, are significantly enhanced.

What's your communication style?

If you are unsure of your dominant style of communicating behaviour, work through the following simple questionnaire. Do not worry if your responses fall into all the different categories; identify with the strongest trend. The mix of responses will help you focus on the specific areas in your style that you may wish to change.

Broadly speaking, if most of your responses fall into the 'Sometimes' category, you may tend to be aggressive or passive/aggressive. If they fall into the 'Never' category, you are certainly passive. If you find that your responses are predominantly in the 'Often' column, you are well on the way to being assertive.

Communication style questionnaire

	Sometimes	Often	Never
1 I feel that I represent myself well in all communications and am respectful of others.	☐	☐	☐
2 My ideas are considered valuable and are often adopted.	☐	☐	☐
3 I am able to say no without feeling guilty.	☐	☐	☐
4 I am able to make complaints without losing my temper.	☐	☐	☐
5 I am able to give feedback to another without causing offence.	☐	☐	☐
6 I can communicate effectively in a group, allowing each member to be heard.	☐	☐	☐
7 I am able to ask for help.	☐	☐	☐
8 I am able to meet my own and others' needs.	☐	☐	☐
9 I can control my temper.	☐	☐	☐
10 People find that I am good at talking through ideas and problems.	☐	☐	☐
11 I am free from disabling stress.	☐	☐	☐
12 I am comfortable with who I am.	☐	☐	☐

Know your worth

We all have basic human rights:

- the right to choose
- the right to 'be'
- the right to be respected
- the right to make mistakes
- the right to say 'no'
- the right to ask for what we want
- the right to ask for what we need.

Understand your fears

It is often our fears that prevent us from developing assertive behaviour. What are yours? For example, they might be: 'I will lose my friends', 'I will make a fool of myself', 'No one will like me any more', 'I will become irritating', or
'.. ' (fill in your own).

Our fears are usually much larger than reality. Face them; they have a habit of shrinking.

Accept yourself for the way you are

It is very easy to put yourself down. We are our own worst critics. In the main, we are:

- **what** we are supposed to be
- **where** we are supposed to be
- **doing** what we are supposed to be doing.

Release all your disappointments and guilty feelings – forgive yourself. Everything that you have done and experienced has brought you to this point of change. *Everything is to play for.*

Decide to change – if you want to

In making the decision to change your behaviour, you may find it helpful to project forward in time and imagine how it would look, and feel, if you were in control of your communication. Compare this to how you feel now.

SUNDAY

MONDAY

TUESDAY

WEDNESDAY

THURSDAY

FRIDAY

SATURDAY

The power of 'imaging' or 'visualizing' cannot be over-stressed. It is a very useful tool for achieving your objectives, whatever they are.

By 'bringing to mind' or 'picturing in your mind's eye' your desired state, you are actually putting images into your subconscious that, ultimately, determine your behaviour. Your subconscious mind can work only in images; it does not understand timescales or conditions. Imagine yourself as you would like to be and your subconscious will work tirelessly to make this a reality. It cannot fail. Keep reinforcing the images time after time, using positive affirmations if this helps (see Monday for more on this) and the old patterns will soon be obliterated and replaced with the new ones that you have chosen.

Old habits die hard, but they do die, with persistence and determination.

TIP *If you continue to behave as you have always behaved, people will continue to treat you as they have always treated you.*

Give yourself permission to succeed – and fail

You are embarking on a journey of transformation.

Sometimes you will succeed on your terms; sometimes you will fail. Try to regard these occurrences with dispassion. They are merely learning experiences. It will not always be easy but it will be rewarding.

By now you should have identified your dominant style of communication and decided whether or not you are completely happy to continue in this vein.

If not, you may have come up with a conditional 'maybe' in response to the desire to change. This is good enough. It will drive your awareness and allow you to choose how to respond in different situations. There may be times when you want to submit, for instance. And there may be times when you feel the need to dominate. Being assertive is about the choice to communicate in the way you feel is most appropriate at the time. Being free to flex your communication style at will is part of being assertive.

If you decide to make changes in the way you communicate and in the way you are perceived by your colleagues, then proceed with enthusiasm; there is much you can gain from the following chapters.

SUNDAY

MONDAY

TUESDAY

WEDNESDAY

THURSDAY

FRIDAY

SATURDAY

Summary

To recap, the different communication styles are broadly divided into the following categories:

 passive   ● assertive

● passive/aggressive   ● aggressive.

These may sound pejorative descriptors but they do convey the underlying motivations of the person using this form of communication.

They are loosely associated with the following characteristics:

● victim   achiever

● manipulator   ● dictator.

Think about how these terms resonate with you. If you have a strong reaction to one or other of them, it may be worth exploring why this is so. Is it something you find distasteful because you feel it is a 'bit close to the truth'?! Try to objectify the way you analyse your own style and try to prevent yourself from judging or criticizing yourself.

Fact-check (answers at the back)

Think about the following questions and use them to build self-awareness and challenge yourself.

1. My dominant style of communication is...
a) Aggressive ❏
b) Passive/aggressive ❏
c) Passive ❏
d) Assertive ❏

2. I am able to be assertive...
a) At will ❏
b) Sometimes ❏
c) Occasionally ❏
d) Never ❏

3. I can flex between communication styles...
a) When I feel it's appropriate ❏
b) With preparation and effort ❏
c) When I want to get something for myself ❏
d) I can't change my style at all ❏

4. I think the assertive style of communication is...
a) Dominating and imposing ❏
b) Manipulative ❏
c) Highly effective ❏
d) For wimps! ❏

5. I believe the advantages of assertiveness is...
a) You can always get what you want ❏
b) You can establish good rapport ❏
c) You can make others feel like losers ❏
d) There are no advantages! ❏

6. When I need to make a customer complaint, I...
a) Apologize profusely for being a nuisance ❏
b) Get angry so that I can fire my complaint boldly ❏
c) Establish the context, the concern and discuss a solution ❏
d) Leave with the product I'm complaining about! ❏

7. When someone comes to me and asks me for advice, I...
a) Give it freely and tell them what to do ❏
b) End up taking on their battle ❏
c) Encourage them to think about how they're going to deal with the situation ❏
d) Avoid getting involved in the first place! ❏

8. There are situations when assertive behaviour is definitely not called for!
a) This statement is true ❏
b) Assertiveness is always called for ❏
c) Communication styles are driven by external situations ❏
d) Communication styles are not dependent upon situations ❏

9. I believe that my personality drives my communication style and...

a) I'm stuck with the communication style that matches my personality ❑

b) I'm an 'introvert' and can never be assertive! ❑

c) I can learn different communication styles regardless of my personality ❑

d) I have to change my personality before I can change my communication style ❑

10. If I could develop more assertiveness, I would benefit by...

a) Getting people to do as they're told by me! ❑

b) Being in charge of my own life ❑

c) Making sure I was in situations that call for assertiveness ❑

d) There would be no benefit to me ❑

MONDAY

TUESDAY

WEDNESDAY

THURSDAY

FRIDAY

SATURDAY

MONDAY

Creating winning scenarios

Creating winning scenarios is the foundation stone for being assertive and being in charge of your own life. This does not mean that you always get your own way, but it does mean that you will be satisfied that you have represented yourself assertively and can live happily (or acceptingly!) with the outcome.

Today's agenda is to bring you that little bit closer to being in control of your own life – asserting yourself in the way you choose. In order to achieve this, we will look at:

- 'winning' language
- positive affirmations
- creative visualization
- building self-esteem.

Those who are adept at turning on assertive behaviour are also quite able to observe their actions, talk themselves through their learning and test the effect of new behaviours. Self-knowledge is the key to taking control of our lives.

Observing, questioning and asking for feedback are vital if we are to succeed.

'Winning' language

'Winning' language is the language of assertive behaviour. It speaks more than mere words to those you communicate with and tells them that you are in control.

Those who recognize this quality in you will nonetheless be hard pressed to say exactly what it is that you are doing to give them this impression. Actually, it is a subtle combination of body language, mental attitude and verbal language.

> **TIP** *It's not what you say that counts; it's the way that you say it.*

The 'winning' qualities of an assertive communicator are:

- the use of 'I' statements
- direct, clear language
- an ability to demonstrate understanding and to empathize ('active listening skills')
- an ability to build rapport and maintain relationships
- good posture, voice and eye contact
- confidence in what they say – no self-effacing comments or profuse apologies!

Direct, clear language

Language can be a very inadequate and clumsy tool for communication. It can also be beautifully simple and, combined with reinforcing messages through the various physical channels of communication (body language), it can be extremely effective and evocative.

Here are some simple rules to help you practise assertive, 'winning', language:

- **Set the scene** by describing – very briefly – what you are referring to: 'When you called a meeting last Friday, I...'
- **Simplicity, clarity and brevity** are key to assertive communication. Do not ramble; you will lose the attention of your audience. Make your point quickly.
- **Take responsibility** for what you are saying. This is done by using the first person. Here are two examples, one negative

and one positive: 'I am unhappy about the way this project is proceeding'; 'I'm delighted with the outcome of this meeting.'

● **Use repetition** if you feel that your message isn't getting across, but restructure your statement the second time.
● **Use silence appropriately** – it can say more than words. Don't be afraid of it; try it out.

Active listening skills

Active listening ranks highly in the league table of communication skills. It enables you to empathize with your audience and build successful relationships. Stated simply, active listening is listening with curiosity; or listening as if you've never heard the other person speak before. When you do this, you will be able to meter your own communication more precisely because you will have homed in on what others are saying without making premature judgements, assumptions or jumping to conclusions.

Good listeners do several things. They...

● **paraphrase** – briefly summarize what has just been said
● **ask 'open' questions** to elicit good information – 'how?' and 'what?' ('why?' can sound whiney or inquisitorial)
● **show an interest** – maintain good eye contact and prompt more communication by nodding from time to time, using encouraging words like 'Yes', 'Ah-ha' and 'Mmm'.
● **give feedback** – reflect back what they believe is being said.

Building rapport and maintaining relationships

Everybody needs to feel liked and valued. Others are likely to be generous in their dealings with you if you manage to develop a healthy rapport. It is a good investment *if done genuinely and generously.* If you do this as a manipulative technique, your motivation will almost certainly be exposed.

Developing good rapport is based on taking an interest in the other party, understanding and remembering what they have said and remembering to acknowledge significant events or achievements.

Body language also plays a part in developing rapport (more of this on Friday).

It sometimes helps to write down others' activities as well as your own if you are forgetful. However, you will soon find that if you manage to develop active listening skills, you will start to remember things more reliably. This is because you will have been concentrating on what the other person has been saying, and you will have heard yourself summarize the main points.

> *Hearing yourself say something really does help you to remember. Talking to yourself is not a sign of madness; it is a valuable aide-memoire.*

Good posture, voice and eye contact

It is somewhat galling to note that only about 7 per cent of what you say (the words you use) contributes towards the message you are trying to convey.

Much more of the message – 38 per cent – is carried in your voice. This includes tone, pitch, speed and the quality of your voice.

The remainder, some 55 per cent, is conveyed by your body – mostly the eyes. This is why communicating on the telephone or via email can be so misleading. Messages through these media have a tendency to take on a life of their own. Meaning can become distorted when the visual channel of communication is removed. Without the visual cues, it is sometimes difficult to interpret messages accurately and misunderstandings can occur. If read without the visible signals that accompany humour, for instance, messages can sound aggressive or sarcastic. It is important, therefore, to remember this and forestall any likely misinterpretation by signposting or symbolizing humorous remarks.

Good posture and an upright walk look good and convey confidence. Slouching or shuffling along gives completely the opposite impression. Try walking towards yourself in front of a mirror or catch a glimpse of yourself in a shop window. Notice the difference when you try to improve the way you move.

Assertive body language will be covered more fully in Friday's lesson. There are several simple rules to consider for the time being:

- **Stand or sit proud** – taking up as little space as possible conveys lack of confidence or weakness
- **Gesture appropriately** – gestures can help to convey a message when used sensibly. Try not to overdo it, however; a lot of extravagant gesturing can be very distracting
- **Don't fidget** – this will make you appear nervous, as no doubt you are if you are fidgeting!

The use and quality of your voice will affect the other person's perception of what you are saying.

A high-pitched, whiney voice, for example, conveys a 'victim' message: 'I'm really rather weak and pathetic and I'm throwing myself on your mercy!' This style of voice can also sound spoilt and petulant.

By contrast, a loud, deep voice delivering words like machine-gun fire sounds incredibly aggressive.

Notice your own style of vocalization. Would you like to change it?

The optimum style – if there really is such a thing – is a calm pace, pitched mid-range with good intonation and clearly enunciated words. It's not always appropriate, of course, but it does for most eventualities.

To communicate assertively, you must maintain good *eye* contact. Aim to maintain almost constant eye contact while you are listening to another person. It is not so easy, indeed it can be actively disconcerting, to maintain constant eye contact while you are talking, so strike a comfortable balance between looking into and away from the other's eyes.

Your eyes will help in the expression of your message and they will no doubt be on the move much of the time. However you decided to use them, return your glance regularly to the other person's eyes throughout the delivery of your message to pick up how they are feeling about what you are saying.

It is worth noting that, if your body language is out of phase with your words, any hidden agenda will immediately become apparent – if not precisely what it is, at least the fact that you have one!

Confidence in what you say

Confidence is fine if you have it, but most unassertive people are sadly lacking in this department. However, here are some useful tips that you can learn to incorporate in your repertoire very easily.

- **Say what you mean and mean what you say** – be succinct and to the point.
- **Never apologize** – unless you sincerely mean it, then do it only once. (Notice how politicians and business leaders almost never apologize. Are we really convinced that they never make mistakes?)

- **Don't claim to be a fool to compensate for feeling a fool.** We often do this to prompt a contradiction. One of the dangers of this strategy is that you will be believed!

Positive affirmations

Used in the right way, positive affirmations can be enormously helpful. They are designed to retrain the brain to think about ourselves differently.

If we have a poor self-opinion (usually as a result of a series of childhood experiences), then as soon as we suffer a loss of confidence, we will return to these experiences and the feelings they engendered. It will take repeated effort to overcome this tendency and to replace it with something more positive.

For some people, positive affirmations can be very helpful in this process.

Positive affirmations are constant repetitions of a belief we wish to install in our brains to replace the less healthy beliefs we have grown up with.

Positive affirmations must be constantly repeated: if you think how long you have lived with your own negativity, just think how often you will have to repeat a desired belief before it will outweigh, and triumph over, the negative belief that is so firmly lodged in your brain.

How to reprogram your brain

Every time we have a thought, an electrical impulse sets off along a particular route through the brain. After this same thought has been through the mind many times, a physical path becomes etched in the brain. This will deepen with every thinking of the thought. If this happens to be a negative or undermining thought, it will colour what you believe about yourself and project to others. A new path must be created, therefore, that is even deeper, and easier, for the thought to follow – the path of least resistance. This can be achieved through positive affirmations.

Say your positive affirmations every day, like a mantra, and eventually you will find that you have reprogrammed your brain and installed a healthier belief.

There are several rules for designing positive affirmations.

● They must be in the present – 'I am...'
● They must *not* be conditional – 'When I... then I will...'
● They must *not* be undermined – hidden message: 'Who am I trying to fool with all this stuff anyway?!'
● They must be about *you*; nobody else.
● They must be spoken out loud – in private if you wish, but it is important to *hear* yourself say them.

Examples of good affirmations are:

● 'I can handle it.'
● 'I am professionally competent.'
● 'I am a valuable and capable member of the team.'

Creative visualization

Creative visualization is an extremely powerful technique for 'seeing' and 'fixing' your far-distant goals in your mind's eye and for planning and rehearsing the execution of the tasks that lead to the achievement of your goals.

As we have already said, the subconscious mind works in images, and when these are clear, it will work tirelessly to turn these images into reality.

What you need for effective creative visualization is a starting point, and an end point. That is to say, you need to understand your current situation completely and notice how far away you are from reaching your goal.

This is not a negative exercise; it is an unemotional and non-judgemental appraisal to enable you to take realistic, positive action and to measure your progress.

Picture your goal

Once you have isolated and fully understood your current situation, you must then form a very clear image of your goal and 'see', 'feel' or 'sense' it. Imagine it from a detached point of view, as if you were watching a film of yourself. Imagine it every way you can until you have a precise picture. Do not dismantle this picture; hold it clearly in your mind. Return to it regularly so that it becomes reinforced, time and again.

Set some time aside for this visualization so that you can build its strength over time. Do not try to hurry the achievement of your goal. Your subconscious will take the strain between your current situation and your desired state and will work to transform the first image into the second.

This method of achieving what you desire is infallible when done diligently. Indeed, you will probably have some personal experience of a time when you did this instinctively; when you desired something so badly, and so clearly, that you managed to bring it to reality.

Try it with big desires and small, but make sure that they are yours and no one else's. You will not be able to use this technique to manipulate others to do what you want!

Seven steps to creative visualization

In summary, here are the basic steps to effective creative visualization – a method that assertive people adopt without even thinking about it:

1 Notice your current situation and your distance from the goal.
2 Develop a clear image of your goal.
3 Breathe it, feel it, smell it, examine it from all angles.
4 Plan and execute your first and second steps only.
5 Do something else and leave your subconscious to work on the next stage undisturbed. Do not interfere, and do not undermine your images. The next steps will come to you in their own time.
6 Return to reinforce the image of your goal and observe your current position regularly – but not too often; the process needs time to work undisturbed.
7 Finally, trust the process; it will work.

Planning and rehearsing the tasks that have to be performed before reaching your goal are like 'mini' creative visualizations. Each step can be treated in the same way as those listed above for a major goal. Never plan more than two steps ahead, however, as the path your subconscious mind leads you down may be different from the one you expect. Follow it though: it will probably be more creative and more effective than your conscious mind.

If you have no clear idea of the tasks, don't worry; they will pop into your mind when the moment is right.

When you have executed the tasks in your mind's eye, you will find that the ease with which you perform them in reality will be truly remarkable.

TIP *Once you have a clear idea of your goal, everything you do and every decision you make will bring you closer to this goal.*

Building self-esteem

Self-esteem, as opposed to ego, is very difficult to recapture once it is lost. Self-esteem is a measure of how you value yourself, and it is built up from your first breath – or, as in many cases, it is destroyed by damaging experiences or relationships. It is one of the most helpful personal qualities that you can possess because from it stems the belief that you are worthy and able to succeed.

Sometimes people try to camouflage their low self-esteem by portraying excessive confidence. This is just 'noise' used to drown out their feelings of vulnerability and inadequacy. Don't be fooled or intimidated by this. Recognize it as a human solution to intolerable emotional discomfort. In this way, the threat of what appears to be a very confident person will disappear and you will be able to meet them on an equal footing.

Using some of the techniques described above can help to build self-esteem and confidence, but there is no substitute for knowing yourself and knowing the areas in which you are

SUNDAY
MONDAY
TUESDAY
WEDNESDAY
THURSDAY
FRIDAY
SATURDAY

most likely to excel. There is nothing so powerful as a series of successes to lead you towards the establishment of a healthy self-esteem, so plan for them.

Here are some thoughts for you to consider when trying to raise the level of your self-esteem:

- **Let go of being responsible for those around you** – take responsibility for your own choices and feelings.
- **Don't take yourself too seriously** – once you lose your sense of humour, you have lost control.
- **Let go of your 'mad' self-perceptions** – in your rational mind you will know what these are.
- **Know yourself** – understand what is blocking your progress, usually fear of failure, or guilt that you are not good enough.
- **Nurture yourself** – give yourself treats.

Summary

Today you were offered some tips and techniques to enable you to be assertive and to be seen to be in charge of your own thinking and actions. Don't diminish the importance of these tools. If you practise them often, they will become second nature to you and you will soon reap the rewards of your efforts.

Soon your colleagues will notice that you are more decisive, effective and confident. This is excellent news for those who are managing or leading a team.

Remember the following. Project a positive image by:

- adopting 'winning language'
- using body language to reinforce your messages
- developing a positive mental attitude
- listening actively
- building rapport through empathy.

All this will lead to a healthy self-esteem.

Please note, there is no danger of losing your personality by doing these exercises. Your personal style will continue to distinguish you among your colleagues – even if they too are successful at being assertive. Indeed, you will feel freer to express your individuality as you become more comfortable with your powers of assertion.

SUNDAY

MONDAY

TUESDAY

WEDNESDAY

THURSDAY

FRIDAY

SATURDAY

Fact-check (answers at the back)

Think about the following questions and use them to build self-awareness and challenge yourself.

1. Winning language is the hallmark of assertive communication. When I use winning language, I should...
a) Use lots of 'I' statements ❏
b) Tell people of all my successes ❏
c) Ensure I come out on top ❏
d) Find ways to undermine others' efforts ❏

2. Active listening is a powerful tool for communication. When I listen actively I should...
a) Look down and stay quiet ❏
b) Get involved and anticipate what's about to be said ❏
c) Ask open questions and remain curious about the answers ❏
d) Remain actively involved in my own tasks or thoughts while listening to the other person speak ❏

3. I know I have built good rapport when...
a) I have succeeded in getting my message across ❏
b) The person I am talking to leaves with lots of tasks ❏
c) I have convinced the other person of my point of view ❏
d) I have learned something new about the person I'm communicating with and have shown empathy ❏

4. Good body language involves...
a) Lots of gestures to underline the message I'm delivering ❏
b) Sitting on the edge of my seat to show enthusiasm and interest ❏
c) Gazing into the other person's eyes for the duration of the conversation ❏
d) Alignment between the physical and the verbal message ❏

5. I use the technique of creative visualization when...
a) I want to convince others of my good idea ❏
b) I'm bored in a meeting and need entertainment ❏
c) I want to define my own goals ❏
d) I'm designing my PowerPoint presentations ❏

6. I use positive affirmations when...
a) I want to reward someone for their good performance ❏
b) I'm trying to convince myself that I have confidence ❏
c) I'm wanting to transform the negative beliefs I hold about myself ❏
d) I want to get my own way, no matter what else is going on ❏

7. Positive affirmations...
a) Work whether I believe in them or not ❑
b) Work when I put them far enough in the future to give them time to come true ❑
c) Work when I speak of them as if they are true now ❑
d) Don't really work – they're just a gimmick! ❑

8. Being assertive demands that I...
a) Take full responsibility for my decisions ❑
b) Get my own way ❑
c) Am never aggressive or passive ❑
d) Can be relied upon to fight others' battles ❑

9. Assertive people are...
a) Extraverted ❑
b) Loud and gregarious ❑
c) Bullies ❑
d) People with a a healthy self-esteem ❑

10. The ability to be assertive is dependent upon...
a) My personality ❑
b) My levels of confidence ❑
c) A desire to dominate ❑
d) A belief in myself ❑

SUNDAY

MONDAY

TUESDAY

WEDNESDAY

THURSDAY

FRIDAY

SATURDAY

TUESDAY

Dealing with the 'negative'

SUNDAY
MONDAY
TUESDAY
WEDNESDAY
THURSDAY
FRIDAY
SATURDAY

We are constantly challenged by the stresses and strains of life. Finding strategies to manage these in a balanced way may well be the key to feeling happy, healthy and in control. Not only are these stresses and strains to do with the mechanics of living, but also they are to do with the people and situations we encounter. This could be anything from an overcrowded train of tired commuters on a hot day to a curmudgeonly shopkeeper who won't listen to our complaint. It is hard to recover from getting off on the 'wrong foot' but, with awareness and determination, it is possible to turn these events around and protect ourselves from getting swept up in other people's negativity.

Today you will learn some techniques for negotiating your way through this most difficult of territories. To do this, we are going to look at:

● handling anger – yours and others'
● resolving conflict
● giving and receiving critical feedback
● saying no
● handling rejection and failure.

Handling anger – yours and others'

Most of us have an innate fear of anger. This may be a throwback to our childhood years when we felt powerless and vulnerable, or to our more primitive state when we perceived the threat of marauders or predators. When we encounter anger, therefore, our bodies tend to react by preparing us for 'fight or flight' – rapid heartbeat, rapid breathing, an increased supply of blood to the muscles – all as a result of the release of adrenalin into the bloodstream. This is the natural defence mechanism that 'kicks in' when we are threatened, and, at the right time, it is a life-saver. Sometimes, the same set of physiological responses results in a 'freeze' response when we stay stock-still, full of nervous tension, in the hope that the danger will disappear without it noticing us.

In most modern situations, however (on the road or at work, for example), these reactions are inappropriate and unhelpful, and it would benefit us if we learned to override them by reducing our fear and increasing self-understanding and self-control.

What is anger?

Anger is just energy. It will be directed by an angry person indiscriminately at objects or at people. It is like a heat-seeking missile looking for a target and it needs to be deflected, damped or avoided.

The thing to remember when *you* are at the receiving end of someone's anger is that it is not you that has precipitated the anger, but some action or stance that you have taken which has struck an unhappy chord with them. You are still an acceptable human being with rights. The anger you are fielding has risen as a result of the other person's conditioning – sometimes unreasonable conditioning. The same is true of your own anger, of course.

One method for dealing with another's anger – in all but pathological cases – is to remove your personal investment from the situation. View it dispassionately and observe its nature while letting it burn itself out. Don't fuel it.

Try to identify the source of the anger by listening carefully to what is being said – or SHOUTED. You may find that the angry person feels criticized, unimportant, thwarted, hurt – any number of emotions. This will give you a clue as to how to proceed.

If you are still struggling, ask questions to clarify your understanding but try not to be patronizing.

If you are in a public place and you feel embarrassed, just remember that you are the one in control at the moment and that it is the other party that is drawing attention to themselves – and they will, of course; we are a sensation-seeking society.

Once the heat has died down, communicate your understanding of the situation from the other's point of view and negotiate a way forward or a resolution.

If you feel that it is important to douse the anger rapidly, a useful technique to adopt is to match the energy being expended. This is done by making a loud proclamation such as 'I UNDERSTAND WHY YOU ARE SO UPSET and I would feel exactly the same if I were you, but...' As you proceed with your comment, you can drop the pitch of your voice and start to take control.

As an observer, you can often hear when the heat is rising in a situation because voices tend to increase in volume and pitch and words are delivered like bullets.

Try not to be tempted to use 'reason'. The purpose of reasoning is to get the other to agree that their behaviour is unreasonable, and nobody wants to do that when they are at fever pitch. This will obviously build resentment. Reasoning can be a passive/aggressive stance as it attempts to lure the other into a submissive position.

When you feel angry yourself, try the distancing technique. (Deep breathing or counting to ten helps some people.) You can observe your own behaviour quite dispassionately with practice. The observations you make of yourself will contribute enormously to your self-knowledge if you can do it honestly. You will reap untold rewards in your ability to communicate assertively if you can develop the presence of mind to lower your energetic response to a situation and ask yourself 'Are things going to be resolved if I get angry?' If the answer is no, try calming yourself and think of something else.

Here is a checklist for helping you to cope with anger:

- Distance yourself – don't take others' anger personally.
- Understand the cause of the anger by listening and observing carefully.
- Say little or nothing until the anger has died down.
- Respect yourself and the other party; you still both have rights.
- Once a certain degree of tranquillity has been achieved, demonstrate understanding by acknowledging the other's viewpoint – not the same thing as agreeing with it (don't use reason).
- Negotiate a way forward.
- If all else fails, walk away. This is another way of respecting yourself.

Resolving conflict

For the purposes of clarity, conflict is separated from anger, although one can sometimes lead to the other.

Conflict can be invisible, insidious and elusive, particularly with those of the *passive/aggressive* persuasion. It can lead to an impasse, a block which is extremely difficult to move. We have seen many such conflicts in the industrial quarter with unresolved disputes leading to the destruction of organizations or an entire industry.

Conflict can also be clear, reasonable and helpful. Used positively, it can sharpen the mind, increase understanding and lead towards a very satisfying and creative solution.

Many of the techniques for dealing with conflict are similar to those used for dealing with anger. The issues may be more complex because the two opposing positions are often well thought out and rehearsed in advance. The goals of the two parties may at first appear totally different and incompatible. This is rarely the case in reality, however.

Here is a checklist for resolving conflict:

- Establish the desired outcome and priorities for both parties.
- Acknowledge and appreciate the other's position.
- Discuss the points of mutual agreement to establish rapport.
- Compromise on issues that are not central to the desired outcome.
- Identify and clarify those points that are left unresolved.
- Delve for deeper understanding by questioning thoroughly and listening carefully.
- Negotiate a resolution or agree a plan for the next step.

Giving and receiving critical feedback

This is always difficult territory. We usually give critical feedback badly because we are not very good at receiving it.

Giving critical feedback

Giving early critical feedback prevents a bad situation developing into dreadful one.

Here is a guide to giving feedback which may be helpful:

- Be considerate and, above all, be private.
- Don't 'pussyfoot' around – have confidence in what you want to say.
- Take responsibility for the feedback; don't do it because you have been cajoled into doing so and don't base it on rumour or hearsay.
- Make sure that the feedback is based on the behaviour you would like to see changed, not on the personality of the individual.
- Use positive body language (see Friday).

Critical feedback may be given on the back of what is called a 'positive stroke'. For instance: 'I liked the way you handled that call and it might portray better customer service if you used their name.' This is often called the 'feedback sandwich' and, because it is so well known, people often wait for the 'kick' after they've received praise. Try to be sensitive to the individual you're giving feedback to and avoid being formulaic.

Receiving critical feedback

None of us enjoys receiving critical feedback. Indeed, most of us are looking for a confirmation that we are liked and accepted the way we are. However, if we put our vulnerabilities behind us for a moment, it really can be very helpful to hear how others perceive our behaviour or our work. We are then in a better position to make the desired adjustments – if we feel that they are valid.

Sometimes we may feel that the feedback is unfair. If this is the case, try to retain your dignity, state your disagreement and move on. Try not to argue for yourself; you will not convince anybody and you will hand your power straight to the person giving the feedback.

Here is a quick checklist for receiving critical feedback:

- Attend carefully to what is being said.
- Judge for yourself if it is valid; if not, disregard it and move on.
- Do not argue; you will only draw attention to your vulnerabilities.

If you are unfortunate enough to be criticized in public, a dignified reaction will elicit a disproportionate amount of respect from observers while the standing of the person giving the feedback will be severely diminished.

Saying no

We are rewarded with masses of praise when we acquiesce to another's request. This is not surprising as, in doing so, we have taken responsibility for somebody else's task or burden. By comparison, the emotional reward for saying no is somewhat barren.

We are often made to feel guilty and mean when we say no. This is a form of manipulation, a last-ditch attempt to make us change our mind and co-operate after all.

Dealing with this requires a particular kind of resilience. It helps if you really do believe that it is perfectly acceptable to make choices according to your own set of priorities, values and beliefs. This does not mean to say that you need always say no just to prove that you are in control of your own decisions. What it does mean is that you *can* say no.

Here is a list of useful tips that you can use when wishing to say no:

- Really mean it – if you don't, it will probably show and the person making the request will probe and prise until you change your mind. You do not have to give reasons for saying no.
- If you want to think about your response, say 'I will get back to you,' or 'I need some time to think about this.' This is your right – who is doing whom the favour?
- Don't milk the apology, wring your hands anxiously or overplay the excuses.
- You may be able to offer a compromise solution.

Handling rejection and failure

It is very difficult to separate rejection and failure because they are so intrinsically linked. They can bring despair and dejection, a feeling of foolishness, of being unworthy and so many other negative emotions.

Accepting that this is the case for so many of us, the healthy thing to do is to learn from these emotions, work with them and view them from a more positive perspective. This may sound trite and unhelpful, but with a bit of determination your perceived failures and consequent feelings of rejection will disappear into humorous anecdotes: 'Did I tell you about the time when I asked the Chairman if he was authorized to be in the building?!'

Try not to confuse your self-worth with one fleeting, albeit negative, experience. To be too harsh on yourself is unhelpful and, at a time like this, you need all the forgiveness and understanding you can get – even if it has to come from you.

One useful tactic you may like to employ to avoid the feeling of total defeat is to make a series of contingency plans. In thinking through possible, probable or even improbable scenarios that are likely to tarnish your reputation, you can spend some useful time preparing coping strategies. In this way, you can redeem yourself rapidly and divert the destructive feelings of rejection and failure into a more positive arena.

Don't dwell for too long on the negative; you may find you have creatively visualized something you would rather not come true.

These tips may be helpful as part of your survival package:

- Try not to link your own worth to negative experiences.
- Never be short of alternatives – develop contingency plans.
- Know that the significance of negative experiences changes with time.
- Try to distil some learning from the experience – it will protect you next time.
- Be kind to yourself.

The whole gamut of negative experiences and emotions are uncomfortable at best but, having conquered your fear and having successfully dealt with a few difficult situations, you will soon re-educate your reflex reactions to co-operate with the way you would rather be.

Developing a balanced view on these matters will make you much stronger because you won't be trying to avoid issues; instead, you will be making choices and following them through confidently.

You are not invincible, so try not to get over-zealous in your enthusiasm to tackle negativity. There definitely are situations that are best avoided because there can be no victor in their resolution. Anger that turns to physical violence is an irrational act and therefore cannot be approached in a rational way. In these circumstances, self-preservation is the key and, if your body prepares you for flight – do it!

Summary

In summary, what we have been dealing with today is 'negative energy'. When this is understood, fear can evaporate, and this energy can be transformed into a positive outcome for everyone. Negative energy is frightening and difficult because it 'pings' us back into a vulnerable position and gives rise to fears of survival. These primitive responses are hard-wired into our brains and still operate, whether the trigger is imaginary or real.

Being able to identify with another human being caught in the grip of fury may enable us to empathize with their plight, and in so doing enable us to behave generously.

It is worth noting that behaving assertively, as you would be if you managed to control an angry exchange without destruction to either party's, or your own, esteem, is not always the 'right' solution. Being passive may be the best response if, for instance, you're being mugged. Or dominating aggressively might suit an emergency situation, where people need direction from someone in charge.

Being assertive means that you can make choices about how and what you communicate. It puts you in the driving seat of your own relationships and allows you to remain robust and confident – yet not insensitive. You can achieve this 'healthy self-esteem' if you're prepared to be conscious and make some disciplined changes to your behaviours.

SUNDAY
MONDAY
TUESDAY
WEDNESDAY
THURSDAY
FRIDAY
SATURDAY

Fact-check (answers at the back)

Think about the following questions and use them to develop your skills in managing negative energy.

1. When someone is angry, it's best to...
a) Reason with them ❏
b) Shout back with equal ferocity ❏
c) Submit to their power and escape at the earliest opportunity ❏
d) Stand firm and try to understand what's going on for them ❏

2. When someone is angry with me, I should...
a) Freeze and submit to their request ❏
b) Fight and endeavour to win the battle ❏
c) Flee from the situation in the hope that they'll calm down ❏
d) Sum up the situation and respond in a way that will lead to a win/win ❏

3. Here is a checklist for resolving conflict. Which is the *incorrect* item on the list?
a) Acknowledge and appreciate the other's position ❏
b) Compromise or relinquish issues that are not central to the desired outcome ❏
c) Seek deeper understanding by questioning and listening thoroughly ❏
d) Ensure that you retain the 'upper hand' by withholding your trump card ❏

4. When you wish to give critical feedback, how should you back up your comments?
a) Canvas others' opinions and add these to your feedback ❏
b) Remind people of their ingrained and persistent personality faults ❏
c) Wait until the situation becomes intolerable and then launch your arsenal ❏
d) Base it on your observations only and focus it on the person's behaviour ❏

5. When you say no, what should you be aiming to feel?
a) Guilty ❏
b) That you're being unreasonable ❏
c) That people will dislike you ❏
d) Fine saying no ❏

6. When you go into a situation that you feel may be 'negative', how should you prepare yourself?
a) Just go in and hope for the best ❏
b) Go in guns blazing to ensure that no one gets the better of you ❏
c) Think about the tensions and tell yourself that they are not personal ❏
d) Try to keep as quiet as possible in the hope that no one notices you ❏

7. When you receive challenging or negative feedback, how should you respond?

a) Tell the person who's giving you feedback to mind their own business ❏

b) Thank the person and tell them you'll think about what they've said ❏

c) Argue your case. No one is going to criticize you and get away with it! ❏

d) Say sorry and that you'll not do it again ❏

8. When handling someone's anger, it is best to...

a) Shout at them to calm them down ❏

b) Reason with them and get them to see they're wrong ❏

c) Appraise the situation and see if you can discover what's causing the problem ❏

d) Leave them to it until their anger burns out ❏

9. When you feel rejected, you should...

a) Blame yourself for being 'wrong' ❏

b) Tell yourself the other person doesn't know what they're doing ❏

c) Try to retain your self-esteem and recognize this is not to do with 'you' ❏

d) Tell them you don't want to be included anyway! ❏

10. Active listening can be done while...

a) Texting friends ❏

b) Emailing work colleagues ❏

c) Being curious about the other person's situation ❏

d) Interrupting enthusiastically to build the conversation ❏

WEDNESDAY

Creating a positive impression

There are many possibilities for making the best of yourself and creating a positive first impression. Today we will be examining some of the techniques that can be adopted to achieve this. They include:

- creating a positive first impression
- developing assertive interviewing skills
- building confidence.

In order to create a good first impression, you will need to manage the perceptions of others. These will be formed through the persona you project – which may, of course, be light years from the one you revert to in private.

It is worth remembering that when people form a perception of us they act as if this is the truth. Once formed, this 'truth' is seldom revisited and reviewed. Rather, it is taken on board as fact and the 'impression-holder' orientates their behaviour towards us accordingly. If we have inadvertently created an unhelpful or misleading first impression, this can give us a long-term problem as people are often reluctant to discuss their initial thoughts about us.

If we attempt to 'manipulate' the perceptions people have of us, it may be hard to sustain – and we may feel alien to ourselves as we are not being authentic. We will explore this phenomenon further today.

Creating a positive first impression

The first opportunity we have to create a good impression is at an initial meeting or during an interview for a job.

It is undoubtedly true that human beings are judgemental. We generally look for similarities in those we are meeting for the first time because this reinforces us as individuals and gives us common ground to explore. We are less tolerant of those who take diametrically opposed views to our own or who live by a different set of values.

When meeting someone for the first time, you can be absolutely sure that they have this lightning ability, as you do, to sum you up in something under ten seconds and be utterly convinced that their powers of perception are completely accurate! You have only these very few seconds, therefore, to create the impression of your choice.

Very often our first impressions are proven wrong in the long run. However, it does take a huge amount of time and effort to dismantle a first impression and substitute it for a more accurate one.

Let us now examine the many factors that go in to creating a first impression:

- appearance
- size, mobility and national origin
- handshake
- gait, body language
- voice, accent, speech pattern, speech impediment, tone, etc.

Judgements will be made on a combination of some or all of the above factors before we start saying anything of consequence.

We will look at these factors one by one.

Appearance

In order to decide how to make your impact, you must first determine what impression you wish to create. An obvious point, perhaps, but often neglected.

Here are some factors to consider when planning your impact at a job interview:

- the culture of the target organization
- the nature of the job
- the note you wish to strike with your clothes:
  - a large amount of bright **colour** can be overpowering
  - **style** can be appropriate/conventional/unconventional
  - **accessories** – shoes, ties, scarves, hairstyle, hair colour, jewellery, bags, belts and briefcases all contribute to the overall impression.

If you decide to create the image of a non-conformist – beware. Although this gives you greater freedom and enormous scope for painting a very individualistic picture, it is a high-risk strategy, especially in a conventional environment. The question to ask yourself is: How seriously do I want this job?

Size, mobility and national origin

There is very little most of us can do about our size, degree of mobility or origin. Unfortunately, it is undeniable that these factors strongly influence a first impression, so be aware of them and quickly remove any concern that the interviewer may have.

If you think that you may encounter some form of prejudice, be proud and be direct. This is very disarming and will soon put the issue (if any) into the background, leaving you with the upper hand. It will also create a relaxed atmosphere for further discussion. This is an essential step to take if there is any possibility that the interviewer will perceive a physical barrier to your suitability for the job, so deal with likely issues honestly and without apology, then move on.

Here are some examples that illustrate how an interviewee can remove prejudice at the outset:

- 'Although you can see I am very large, I would like to reassure you that this does not hinder my performance.'
- 'I would like you to know that my physical restrictions have enabled me to develop other skills to an extremely high level.'

Handshake

Within a split second of meeting someone for the first time, we are there, proffering our hand as the best etiquette has taught us. There are many varieties of handshake, some desperately disconcerting, others businesslike and almost unremarkable. The conclusions we draw from a handshake are out of all proportion to its significance. However, getting it wrong puts a large obstacle in the way of creating a good impression.

We have all experienced the limp handshake... the 'tip of fingers' handshake... the ferocious 'bone-breaker'... the sweaty handshake... and the 'won't let go' handshake...

The model way to shake someone's hand is to:

- offer an open hand, your palm facing towards theirs
- look the other party in the eye and smile
- take a firm hold of their hand and shake it up and down once or twice (no more)
- release.

Gait, body positioning

Body language will be dealt with in much greater detail on Friday, but as we are on the subject of first impressions, it is necessary to touch on the matter here.

How you enter a room, move towards a greeting, walk or sit, all go towards forming an early impression.

Assertive behaviour can also be demonstrated non-verbally in the following three ways:

1 moving assertively (including the handshake)
2 sitting assertively
3 use of the voice (yes, it is considered to be a non-verbal mode of communication).

Moving assertively: when preparing to enter a room, knock firmly on the door and wait for a response. Once you have been asked to 'come in', open the door fully, step in and close the door behind you. Walk confidently into the room towards the greeting, hand at the ready.

Don't be timid. If you tap lightly on the door, no one will hear and you won't be asked to 'come in'. Then you will probably be anxious and uncertain – you have sabotaged yourself.

If you creep round the door, hug the wall and shuffle hesitantly towards the greeting, you will appear insipid and lacking in confidence. This is typical passive behaviour. However, if you stride in, throw your briefcase down and sit without being invited to do so, it will not appear confident, as you might hope, but aggressive.

Sitting assertively: sit straight and tend to lean slightly forward. This gives the impression of meeting someone part way on their territory and looks interested and enthusiastic.

If you slouch or lean back on your shoulder blades with your bottom pivoting on the edge of the chair, you will appear uninterested and disrespectful.

Contrarily, if you sit huddled and small with your toes pointing together and your hands gripped firmly between your knees, you will look childlike and helpless.

Voice: there are many dimensions to your voice, most of which are difficult to control, such as a national or regional accent, a speech impediment or the quality of your vocal cords.

Some of the vocal properties that you can control are the clarity of your speech, the pitch, the tone and the speed of delivery.

The words that you use, the grammatical patterns you favour when constructing your sentences, and the way you reinforce what you are saying with your hands all have a direct bearing on how you will be perceived, albeit unconsciously. More of this later.

Creating a positive first impression – invisibly

Our first contact with a person may be through email, by letter or on the telephone.

Because these modes of communication are stripped of the normally abundant visible information such as appearance, style, movement and, in the case of the written word, voice, it becomes all the more important to make the most of what is left. 'Remote' modes of communication are still filled with opportunities for creating a good first impression.

We will look at the potential of three forms of 'remote' communication.

Email

Email is quite an informal mode of communication with a tradition for grammatical shortcuts and abbreviations. However, most people now offer their email address and invite contact electronically. If you use this channel of communication to create a first impression, ensure that you do so through a high-quality message. Use the attachment facility to carry properly formatted documents that can be printed by the recipient.

Letter

There are significant advantages to making your first impression by letter. When initial contact is made through the written word, you have the luxury of time to plan the impression you wish to create.

Listed below are some useful tips on how to create a good impression by letter:

- Ensure that the quality of the paper and the appearance of the writing are excellent: no spelling mistakes, daubs of correction fluid, colloquialisms or bad grammar.
- Handwritten letters are fine if you possess a 'good hand' that is attractive and legible. Many bad characteristics are associated with poor handwriting. Word-processed letters look very professional, so do use this method if you can.
- Make sure that what you have to say is succinct and to the point. Any information that you give in addition to what is necessary should be carefully chosen.

The telephone

When communicating by telephone, you have the benefit of being invisible so you can get really comfortable with yourself and what you plan to say.

Here are some helpful tips on making a good first impression using the telephone:

- Do not use a mobile.
- Smile when your call is answered; this can be heard in your voice.
- Use a pleasant greeting and state your name and purpose clearly.
- Plan what you are going to say (writing down key words will ensure you cover all the essential points).
- If you are trying to get your thoughts together, pace about if it helps and use gestures.
- If you are interrupted during your call, explain what has happened so that your distraction does not appear rude or offhand.
- Summarize and confirm all agreements verbally so that you can be sure you have understood accurately.
- Establish who will initiate the next contact; if you are anxious, it is as well to take the responsibility for this yourself.

- It is often useful to follow up a telephone conversation with a letter of confirmation.
- If you seem to be listening for a long time, acknowledge what is being said by using terms like 'Ah-ha', 'Mmm' and 'Yes'. Long silences can sound as if you are no longer there or have stopped paying attention
- If you find you need to be assertive, stand up while talking on the telephone; it really does help to convey a feeling of strength.

Assertive interviewing skills

Many specialist books have been written on the subject of 'the interview'. However, today would not be complete without some reference to 'the interview' and how you can manage this assertively.

During a professionally conducted interview, the interviewer should talk for 5–10 per cent of the time only. Ideally, therefore, you will have the remainder of the time to give as much relevant information about yourself as possible.

Your curriculum vitae will have conveyed all the professional, technical and experiential information necessary to determine your suitability for the post. The interview is primarily geared towards finding out whether you will fit in to the culture of the organization and work effectively with the rest of the team.

You will be prompted to give information about yourself through 'open questions'. Listen out for these because they provide you with the opportunity to show yourself in a good light. Examples of open questions are:

- 'What made you decide to...?'
- 'How would you tackle...?'
- 'Explain more about how you...'

They are 'open' because you determine the content and limits of the answer; there are no bounds to them. They give you masses of scope to talk about your approach and your achievements.

'Closed' questions, for comparison, are those such as:

- 'How long did you work for...?'
- 'How many staff were you responsible for at...?'
- 'When did you pass your driving test?'

These questions prompt short, defined responses and, as a consequence, the interviewer has to work extremely hard to extract sufficient information from you to reach a decision.

If you happen to be at an interview where the interviewer asks you 'closed' questions, take the initiative and open them up yourself, saying something like:

- 'Yes, I enjoyed being an apprentice because it gave me an opportunity to...'
- 'I worked for Hobson's Choice for ten years and thoroughly enjoyed it because it developed my ability to...'

Remember, undertake some basic research on the organization and the nature of its business before you attend an interview. Interviewers often ask 'What do you know about this organization?' You can impress easily with a knowledgeable response to this question.

Summary

To close the learning for today, let us look at what creating a positive image is all about – *confidence*.

By adopting some of the techniques and attitudes given to you today, you will soon begin to trust that you are capable of forming and maintaining an image that pleases you. Initially, one small success is all you can ask of yourself. Having this safely behind you will be the beginning of building confidence. Start with something you find relatively easy, and move on to greater things from there.

Good habits, firmly established, are soon drawn into the subconscious where they form the bedrock of your behaviour. When you have progressed this far, you will find that your confidence level has increased significantly and you will be able to draw upon it quite naturally. Once you reach this stage, all your positive experiences will go towards reinforcing this new-found quality in yourself. You will have established a virtuous cycle! Confidence and a healthy self-esteem are priceless assets and, if you are not fortunate enough to possess them naturally, they are well worth working for.

A positive mental attitude is key. Many managers have learned this from the experience of athletes who develop their minds as well as their bodies. Belief in yourself, coupled with professional expertise, will ensure your success.

SUNDAY

MONDAY

TUESDAY

WEDNESDAY

THURSDAY

FRIDAY

SATURDAY

Fact-check (answers at the back)

Think about the following questions and use them to develop your skills in creating a positive impression.

1. What do you need to do to create a positive first impression?
   a) Tell people what you want them to believe of you ❏
   b) Behave authentically, taking account of the context and situation ❏
   c) Act out the person you want to be seen as ❏
   d) Adopt a 'what you see is what you get' approach and leave it to chance ❏

2. Which one of the options below is *incorrect* as a way of making a first impression?
   a) Considering my appearance – appropriate dress and grooming ❏
   b) Building rapport and being congruent with the situation ❏
   c) Demonstrating authenticity and confidence in myself ❏
   d) Acting as if I was the person I want to be ❏

3. Handshakes are very important in creating a first impression. How should you shake someone's hand?
   a) Offer little resistance so that they can determine the strength of the handshake ❏
   b) I dislike shaking hands so try to avoid it ❏

   c) Take the 'firm' approach so that they know you're confident in yourself ❏
   d) My hands are sweaty so I try to minimize contact ❏

4. When entering a room for the first time, perhaps to meet a prospective employer, how can you command the space?
   a) I knock and enter without being invited to show my confidence ❏
   b) I comment on the (good, bad, indifferent) weather immediately to show I'm friendly ❏
   c) I respond confidently to the requests made of me to sit, speak and ask questions ❏
   d) I stand quietly and wait for instructions before I make a move ❏

5. Which one of the statements below is likely to create a *poor* impression when there are no visible channels of communication?
   a) I make sure my written communications are grammatically correct and high quality ❏
   b) I smile on the telephone, knowing that this will be conveyed in my voice ❏
   c) I use texting because it's quick and easy ❏
   d) I make sure my CV is succinct and points towards my capabilities and achievements ❏

6. Interviews that use open questions are designed to check the 'chemistry' between you and your prospective employers. Which statement *incorrectly* defines open questions?

a) They are designed to get you to talk more about yourself ❏
b) They begin with 'Who?', 'What?', 'Where?', 'When?' and 'How?' ❏
c) They are traps that encourage you to say things you don't want to! ❏
d) They are exploratory and encourage you to expand upon your points ❏

7. If you feel that you may possess a barrier to being considered for a new job, how would you diminish it to equal your chances?

a) I'd hope that the interviewer hadn't noticed and say nothing ❏
b) If they mentioned it, I'd deny it was a problem ❏
c) I'd be candid about the perceived barrier and explain why it would not be an obstacle to my suitability ❏
d) I'd point out that it was politically incorrect or illegal to focus on this issue ❏

8. Which statement is incorrect in describing how to communicate assertive behaviour non-verbally?

a) Through posture and well-defined movement ❏
b) By taking every opportunity to stand up and create a physical hierarchy in my favour ❏
c) By sitting slightly forward in the chair to convey engagement ❏
d) By speaking clearly and fluently ❏

9. If you were being interviewed and the interviewer was not asking you the questions you'd like to answer, how would you deal with it?

a) I'd give them a list of questions I'd like them to ask me ❏
b) I'd give feedback to the interviewer that they're not giving me the opportunity to sell myself properly ❏
c) I'd ask if I could outline a project that illustrates my suitability for the role ❏
d) I'd feel disappointed and wish they'd been better at their job! ❏

10. Which statement could endanger my growth in confidence?

a) I could be positive about my capabilities and achievements ❏
b) I could try not taking things too personally ❏
c) I could try envisaging my future successes ❏
d) I could over-act to convey that I really was confident ❏

SUNDAY

MONDAY

TUESDAY

WEDNESDAY

THURSDAY

FRIDAY

SATURDAY

THURSDAY

Being assertive in public

Yesterday we looked at ways of creating a positive impression in one-to-one situations: at a job interview, on the telephone and through the written word.

Today we are going to look at how to develop this transient first impression into a durable professional image. You may like to think of this as your 'brand' image. This will be an amalgam of the characteristics, traits and behaviours that you show to the outside world. If you are to transmit your 'brand' effectively, you will need to be consistent in the way your portray yourself. If you try out new things too often, it will fragment your brand and undermine the progress you've made and the reputation you've established.

To assist you, we will concentrate on your ability to communicate assertively in public, among work colleagues and customers. As you grow in professional stature, you will increasingly find yourself in situations where many pairs of eyes will be watching you. You will be visible to a wider audience.

Much of the assertive behaviour about to be described will be applicable to more than one arena. Here we will focus on three of the most frequently met situations in which your ability to communicate assertively will reap great rewards:

- meetings
- negotiations
- presentations.

Meetings

Meetings are often dominated by the most aggressive members of the group. In these circumstances, passive attendees can feel completely overtaken by events because they feel unable to interject and make their points. Passive types will often revert to passive/aggressive behaviour on such occasions – deafeningly 'loud' body language and more than a few sighs – or they will become silent and resign themselves to the decisions made without their input.

A good chairperson will ensure that the meeting is properly orchestrated and that everyone is given the opportunity to contribute. Often, however, this leadership is sadly lacking and meetings either take on the air of a battlefield or wander off the point and waste a lot of time.

For the purposes of illustrating how to handle meetings assertively, we will look at the worst scenario: that of a disorganized gathering dominated by one or two aggressive types. We will pepper this image with a few passive and passive/aggressive characters who are nursing 'hidden agendas'.

After a few words on how to prepare for a meeting, we will pull the above scenario apart and look at each component individually:

- assertive versus aggressive
- assertive versus passive/aggressive

- assertive versus passive
- assertive versus hidden agenda.

Preparing for a meeting

Before attending a meeting, make sure that you have a copy of the agenda and that you fully understand why the meeting has been called.

Take with you all the supporting information you are likely to need. If you are not clear why a particular item has been included on the agenda, ask beforehand.

Make sure you know where the meeting is being held and get there on time. You will lose credibility if you turn up late, confused or ill poorly prepared, and it will then be much harder to make an assertive and constructive contribution.

Assertive versus aggressive

Let's start by dealing with the aggressive component of the meeting. Aggressive behaviour often works in the short term. It intimidates and controls those who fear it, and many do. However, it is not worth adopting aggressive behaviour as a long-term strategy. Eventually colleagues will get angry.

The demonstrable lack of regard and respect that the aggressive person exhibits will eventually lead to unco-operative and undermining responses. Once commitment has been lost, there is no way forward for the aggressor.

The use of assertive behaviour in these circumstances can, however, draw the aggressor towards a healthier realm of communication. Here's how.

When faced with aggressive behaviour, be calm, breathe deeply and know that others at the meeting will be gunning for you. One word of caution, however: assertive behaviour is about taking responsibility for yourself, not for others; so don't speak for the group, speak for yourself. Use 'I' language.

You may have to field anger, criticism and insults before you can start influencing the communication. Remember, though, that aggressive behaviour is weak behaviour. Be confident; you can handle it.

Here is a checklist for dealing with aggressive behaviour:

- Be calm; listen carefully.
- Take a deep breath and look for an opportunity to speak. If you need to interrupt, try to catch the speaker's eye and indicate your wish to contribute. If the speaker is hell-bent on avoiding eye contact, call their name politely and state your intention to contribute.
- Match the volume of your interruption to the volume of the speaker's voice.
- Once you have successfully entered the dialogue, acknowledge what has just been said, then lead off with a statement such as 'I understand the point you are making, but I feel we could achieve more by...'
- If you are dismissed, repeat your comment in a different way. Repeat yourself assertively until you have been heard.
- Once you have the floor you may find you need to halt a 'return play' interruption. In this case, raise your hand to signal 'stop'. Using the person's name increases the power of your gesture.
- Summarize and confirm your understanding of a point or agreement before moving on.
- If you have not succeeded in making your point, register the fact. For example: 'I know that you are keen to cover a lot of ground in this meeting, but I still feel...'
- Maintain dignity even if you are frustrated, and reassert yourself on a later occasion. Persistence really does win out in the end and you will become more effective each time you attempt assertive behaviour.

Assertive versus passive/aggressive

Passive/aggressive behaviour is 'reluctant victim' behaviour. It attempts to be manipulative. A person may be angry with themselves for giving away their power so they do it with bad grace. This type of behaviour causes bad atmospheres, resentment, embarrassment and confusion. Often, one thing is said but the message is completely different. For instance:

Manager: 'Our best customer has just placed an urgent order; would you mind processing it immediately?'

Sales assistant (sarcastically): 'No, that's fine. I have all the time in the world!'

Passive/aggressive behaviour is thinly disguised. In a meeting it may exhibit itself through overt body language – rolling the eyes heavenward, exaggerated shifting in the chair, or impatient tapping with a pen.

Here are some ideas for dealing with passive/aggressive behaviour:

● Expose the 'hidden' message, whether verbal or non-verbal. For example: 'I see that you are feeling negatively about this. Would you mind discussing your objection openly?'
● Ask for their thoughts on the topic of obvious dispute.
● Listen actively and respond.

The passive/aggressive person has several options when their behaviour is exposed. They can rise to the challenge and redeem themselves; deny sending the message in the first place, claiming that you are paranoid; or get defensive. The first option is obviously the best strategy; the latter two will without fail diminish their standing in others' eyes.

Assertive versus passive

Passive behaviour attempts to engender feelings of sympathy in others. It is as manipulative as passive/aggressive behaviour but it pretends to be virtuous. Passive people have very little self-respect, they do not stand up for themselves and tend to get 'put upon' because they are frightened to say no and be rejected.

A distinguishing characteristic of a passive person is the use of silence. This can sometimes go on for a very long time and usually covers up a running dialogue in their mind which is 'victim' based ('Why are you picking on me?' or 'I wish you would shut up and leave me out of this!').

Dealing with passive behaviour

Dealing with a passive person is not dissimilar to handling someone who is passive/aggressive. First, expose their abdication: 'I am not clear where you stand on this issue; would you tell me what your feelings are?' (Note the use of the 'I' statement and the 'open' question, 'what?')

Match silence with silence. It takes an extremely passive person to remain mute in the teeth of a silent and expectant gaze, especially if everyone at the meeting is engaged in the same tactic. Once they start to talk, use your active listening skills to encourage the flow.

However, if you lose patience with their silence, repeat your comment or try a different approach if you think this will help. If you get to a point of exasperation, inform the passive person that you will have to deduce their feelings if they are not prepared to share them and that you will have to proceed according to your deductions. Invite them to support you in your course of action.

Assertive versus hidden agenda

You will inevitably come across people who play their cards very close to their chest, especially in organizations where internal politics are prominent. In these cultures, people are always on the defensive, protecting themselves from exploitation or disadvantage. Sometimes this fear is imaginary, sometimes it is real, but, whatever the cause, you will need common techniques to deal with it.

Identifying hidden agendas

You will probably be able to identify the 'political animals' among your colleagues because their behaviour will appear inconsistent. They will apparently change their opinion or approach without reason, leaving a trail of confusion and uncertainty behind them. Once this erratic style has caught your attention, look at the interplay of circumstances and try to identify the likely political, and usually personal, gain that is being sought. You may then be close to the real motivation of that person.

Significant coincidences that benefit one individual do not usually occur without some help. Look for coincidences, therefore, and identify the beneficiaries. Coupled with hindsight, the hidden agenda may suddenly be revealed to you and past, previously confusing behaviours will fall into context. This knowledge is useful; it is power. Do not try to tackle the individual. Hidden agendas, by their very nature, can always be denied and you will end up looking paranoid or foolish.

It is probably worth testing your theory by predicting the likely reaction of your colleagues in certain circumstances. If, when these circumstances occur, your prediction proves correct, the hidden agenda is likely to be what you suspected. If not, think again; maybe you *are* paranoid!

Planning your approach

Having understood a colleague's private motivation, you will have a clear picture of where you fit into the pattern of things. This will enable you to plan your own approach. This could be one of avoidance, of course, if you choose not to get caught up in the politics of the organization; or it may be a strategic option – the choice, as always, is yours.

Hidden agendas: checklist

Here is a checklist for identifying a hidden agenda:

- Examine coincidences that benefit one person, or a specific group of people.
- Look out for inconsistent behaviour – this may take the form of an unlikely relationship, non-verbal messages or a sudden and inexplicable abdication of responsibility.
- Put your observations into context using hindsight; this may help you identify the 'hidden agenda' specifically.
- Test your theory as innocuously and as anonymously as possible.
- It is probably best to keep your own counsel; you may be able to do more to your advantage in this way.
- If you are going to tackle someone on their private agenda, be absolutely sure of your ground and that you can handle it in the most assertive way possible.
- Look for a motivation – if you are suddenly flavour of the month with someone who is known to be ambitious, ask yourself why.
- Be vigilant – it would be naive to think that hidden agendas are not being worked out somewhere within your organization.

Negotiations

There are some very simple rules for conducting yourself effectively – and assertively – in negotiations.

Negotiations can fall into several categories. First, there are those taking place in the working environment with one other person such as your boss, a colleague or a member of your staff. Moving up in scale, the meeting room often witnesses negotiations among several colleagues whose views reside in different camps. Then there are those conducted between two opposing parties. When these two parties cannot agree, they may resort to the services of an arbitrator or mediator.

Whatever the situation, whether it is simple problem solving or a full-scale meeting between managers and a trade union, the basic rules for successful negotiating are the same. More often than not, it is merely a question of scale.

Negotiating in practice

Here are the basic steps for negotiating successfully:

● Know exactly what you wish to achieve and be absolutely clear on the level of your, and your opponent's, authority.
● Be assertive and use positive body language.
● Make sure that you understand the other's viewpoint.
● Convey your own viewpoint clearly and state your desired outcome.
● Look for areas of common ground to reinforce mutual interests and to develop a commitment to a satisfactory resolution.
● Listen actively and demonstrate understanding throughout the discussion.
● Never bluff, fudge, manipulate or lie.
● Never offer something you cannot deliver.
● If you are feeling pressured, ask for a recess.
● Communicate your proposals clearly and concisely and establish those of the other party.
● Summarize the areas of difference and explore the extent of these; identify the issues where compromise is possible.
● Having distilled out the main area of contention, discuss any concessions that you are both prepared to make.
● Summarize, agree and confirm in writing

Presentations

Presentations strike fear into the hearts of many managers, whatever their seniority. They are one of the most visible and exposed professional platforms and can leave your image enhanced, intact or in tatters.

Usually you will have advance warning of the requirement to make a presentation and will also, therefore, have time to prepare and practise for the occasion.

The two most important points are: *prepare* and *practise*.

Those who are 'naturals' at making presentations are the exception rather than the rule. Most good presenters are only good because they have invested time in preparation and practice. Everyone can do it if they try – and everyone can enjoy the experience.

There is nothing more satisfying than the glow of success when you step down from the platform having made an excellent presentation. It really is worth investing the time and energy to get it right.

Of course, much has been written on presentation skills, and clearly justice cannot be done to the subject in a few short paragraphs. However, here are a few pointers to help you add this mode of communication to the assertiveness toolkit that you are assembling:

Preparation and practice

- Make sure that you understand the purpose of the presentation.
- Have a clear impression of your audience, their level and their expectations; this will enable you to pitch your presentation correctly.
- Prepare your talk:
  - **beginning** – tell them what you are going to say
  - **middle** – say it
  - **end** – tell them what you have said.
- Most people will retain only about three points.
- Prepare visual aids:
  - **overhead projector slides** – these should be bold, clear and never more than a paragraph long
  - **handouts** – these can contain more detailed information along with copies of your slides. They should be of top quality
  - **35mm slides** – not always an advantage as you have to make your presentation in a darkened room.
  - **PowerPoint** has raised the standard of presentations and the level of expectation of audiences everywhere. Sound and animation features are available, but make sure they add to your message. Also, be comfortable with the technology, especially if you are projecting your presentation from your laptop on to a screen. If you plug in too early, your audience will be able to watch as you search your directory and open up your presentation.
- Prepare a set of cards with keyword prompts, facts or difficult names on them to help you if you are nervous.
- Practise – in front of a mirror, colleagues, friends and family. Make sure that you get the timing right and get your audience to fire awkward questions at you.

Making the presentation

- Wear clean, comfortable and unobtrusive clothes. If you don't, your audience will pay more attention to your attire than to what you have to say.
- Arrive in plenty of time; familiarize yourself with the equipment and check your slides are in the right order.

- Make sure that you have a glass of water handy in case your mouth dries up.
- If you are using torch pointers, telescopic pointers or infrared remote controls – practise (watch out for shake).
- Relax, by whatever means suits you.
- Tell your audience what you expect from them in terms of interruptions, discussion or questions; you may prefer to take these as you go along, or leave them to the end.
- Enjoy your talk but remain vigilant: it is too easy to be drawn into letting your guard down and saying something contentious. If you cannot answer a question, be honest about it and tell the questioner that you will find out and get back to them.
- Try to avoid jokes until you are a skilled presenter.
- Don't talk down to your audience but, equally, don't assume they understand the technicalities of your subject.
- Pause from time to time. This is a performance, and pauses are useful for dramatic effect – and to collect your thoughts.
- Of course, use assertive language and body posture.

Summary

By now you should have started to gather together some useful tools for developing your assertiveness skills. You may have had a chance to practise some of these techniques and found that they really do work. These early successes should increase your confidence and fire your enthusiasm to learn more, take control and have the courage to set your own goals.

Now that we're about two-thirds of the way through the week, it may be worth checking your progress to see where you are with your assertiveness aspirations and what there is still left to do. You could, for example, ask for feedback from one or two of your trusted friends or colleagues.

It is very easy to slip back if something doesn't go according to plan, so find some support to shore you up in these moments.

You might like to write down your experiences and your learning. It will ensure that everything stays conscious, which is where you need it if you are going to take command of your own communication skills.

SUNDAY
MONDAY
TUESDAY
WEDNESDAY
THURSDAY
FRIDAY
SATURDAY

Fact-check (answers at the back)

Think about the following questions and use them to develop your skills in creating a public image.

1. Which statement is *incorrect* in respect of how you should build your brand?
a) I build my brand in group or departmental meetings ❑
b) I build my brand with clients, customers and suppliers ❑
c) I build my brand among my colleagues who have similar expertise to me ❑
d) I don't build my brand, it builds itself ❑

2. When you run meetings, which statement would suggest that you do so unassertively?
a) I keep things to time ❑
b) I leave with clear action points allocated to the appropriate members of the team ❑
c) I tap into the creativity and problem-solving capability of the team ❑
d) I always end up with all the action points! ❑

3. When you've completed a negotiation, what outcome would suggest that you did so assertively?
a) I conceded too much ❑
b) I was not heard or understood ❑
c) I reached a satisfactory win/win solution ❑
d) I do not know or understand the other party's position and goals ❑

4. Which statement about passive/aggressive behaviour is *false*?
a) People agree (unconvincingly) and then take no action – or sabotage the outcome ❑
b) Often, the body language is 'loud' in its message that the person wants to be anywhere but at the meeting ❑
c) Passive/aggressive behaviour uses sarcasm ❑
d) Passive/aggressive behaviour is a contradiction in terms and doesn't exist ❑

5. Which is the *wrong* step to take when you are preparing for a meeting?
a) Make sure everyone knows where the meeting is, what time it's being held and how long it will last ❑
b) Ensure that an agenda has been circulated and forewarn of any preparation that needs to be done ❑
c) Arrange for minutes to be taken, circulated and agreed afterwards ❑
d) Meetings are best when they are called spontaneously to address an emergent issue ❑

6. What is the effect of aggressive behaviour in a meeting? Identify the *false* statement.
a) It derails the purpose of the meeting ❏
b) It adds a drop of excitement to the proceedings and encourages everyone to contribute ❏
c) It may be effective in the short term ❏
d) People may be fearful of the aggressor and fail to contribute ❏

7. When confronting aggressive behaviour, what should you *not* do?
a) Be calm and listen carefully ❏
b) Acknowledge what is being said and offer your own view ❏
c) Argue with the aggressive person and try to convince them they're wrong ❏
d) If your comment is dismissed, come back again in a different way ❏

8. Which strategy is a passive/ aggressive person *unlikely* to use to avoid taking responsibility?
a) They may tell you that you're paranoid ❏
b) They may deny that you read their signals correctly ❏
c) They may feign agreement and sabotage your plan later on ❏
d) They may apologize, tell you that you've read them correctly and take on a different stance ❏

9. In the event of suspecting someone has a hidden agenda, what should you do?
a) Accuse them of trying to 'get one over on you' ❏
b) Mention that you've noticed them trying to win favour with senior people ❏
c) Set up a 'trap' to see if they fall into it ❏
d) Give them feedback on your feelings and ask if they would clarify their motivations ❏

10. What good practice should you adopt as you step into the world of making presentations?
a) Telling 'good' jokes to get the audience laughing and 'on your side' ❏
b) Saying how nervous you are because you hate giving presentations ❏
c) Being technical to demonstrate how much you know ❏
d) Doing rehearsals to get you used to your voice and the timing of your presentation ❏

Body language

The notion of 'body language' has drawn much attention and intrigue. It is tempting to think that words are the most important factor in communicating messages but, as we have seen, words form only a small proportion of the messages that are exchanged. You have only to think of a mime artist who has perfected the art of communication using the body to recognize the truth of this. Also, think of those people who are very still when they communicate. It is sometimes hard to 'read' them clearly and it may lead to misinterpretations or misunderstandings.

Today we will look at the forms of body language that have the most impact on others. This is by no means an exhaustive study of the subject, but it will maximize the effect you can create when you communicate assertively.

The following areas will comprise today's learning:

- assertive body language
- the use of gestures
- developing rapport
- the use of verbal language
- interpreting body language.

Your body really can speak louder than words.

Assertive body language

Because your body conveys such a large proportion of what you are communicating, it is worth concentrating on this area for a short time and considering what it is we convey with our bodies and how we can be sabotaged by them.

It is a useful exercise to 'body-watch' – but try to be discreet. You will notice that when two people are engrossed in riveting conversation, they are completely unaware of their bodies. (Unless the conversation is skirting around sex, of course; in which case we are *very* aware of our bodies!) We use our bodies at the unconscious level to emphasize points or to transmit secondary messages.

Assertive behaviour is distinguished by the continuity between the verbal and the non-verbal. In other words, your body reflects precisely what you are saying when you are in 'assertive mode' – it is congruent with the intention behind your message.

Because of the restricted time and space available here for this topic, we will address only the most potent aspects of body language:

● personal space
● stance
● senses.

Personal space

We all carry around an egg-shaped exclusion zone which varies in size in direct proportion to our circumstances, purpose and level of comfort. As a point of interest, you can usually measure the size of someone's 'egg' by the length of their focal attention.

On an underground train, this is almost zero (people often look glazed or they focus on reading matter); at work, it can extend to include one person or a small gathering of people; at a large presentation, it can reach to the extremities of an entire hall.

Varying the size of the 'egg' is an instinctive part of our behaviour. However, it can be very useful to understand the nature of this 'personal space' so that it can be used to good effect.

Learning point I. *If we do not include people in our personal space, it is almost impossible to influence them.*

Notice how you 'shut down' when someone you dislike comes too close, or someone you're not sure about comes too close too soon. I'm sure that we have all experienced backing away from someone as they repeatedly trespass on our personal territory until the next step takes us through the window or into a cupboard.

Remember, too, a time when you were part of a large audience, and the presenter or entertainer made you feel as if you were the only person in the room. This was because they extended their personal space to include you.

Notice how you use your own space, and how you act differently with family, colleagues and those in authority. As an exercise, practise drawing your space in until its boundaries meet your body. Then try filling a room with your presence by expanding your space. You can do this by changing your focal point and placing your attention on the walls. Accompany this with a visualization of yourself as an extraordinarily confident and influential person.

Learning point II: *The more space you use, the more impact you will have.*

Tall people tend to have a natural advantage because they occupy a large amount of space. Yet they are often shy and withdrawn. This can show in their posture, which may be round-shouldered, or in their gait, which may be 'in-toed'.

Short people, who may not enjoy the same natural impact, can make up for their lack of size by expanding the horizons of their space and adopting a good assertive style. Indeed, a large number of short people are considered to be taller than they are because of this ability, and they have become extremely successful in the process. Unfortunately, their communication style sometimes overcompensates for their lack of physical stature and can become overly aggressive.

There are ways of sitting and standing that look 'big' and carry impact. By adopting some of the following techniques, short people can actually 'grow' in others' perceptions.

Here are some techniques for creating presence:

- **Assertive standing:** stand straight and 'think' tall. Try not to twine your legs around each other or stand with your weight upon one leg. Nothing destroys the image like crumpling on to the floor because you have overbalanced!
- When you wish to **communicate powerfully,** again, stand straight, feet planted firmly on the floor, body centred, hands at your side. If it is hard to push you over physically, it will be hard to push you around verbally.

- **Assertive sitting:** convey confidence by using as much space as possible while sitting. Sit with your body on the diagonal, bottom well back in the chair and lean slightly forward. Sit 'small' and you will be perceived as small.

Stance

Your posture will convey a huge impression, so it is important to get it right.

Everyone will notice someone who stands upright and walks well. This is a good habit to cultivate. It portrays confidence and authority.

Tall people are notorious for stooping and they always say it is because they can't get through the doors. However, it is an enviable gift to be tall; many would give their eye teeth for height – so, if you are tall, duck only when necessary. Stoop when you are young and you will have no choice but to stoop when you are old.

Short people can walk tall, too. In fact, people of under five foot three can look six foot tall if they have good posture. We often confuse confidence for size, so you can make the most of this misconception by cultivating your own personal stature.

Senses

Taking the liberty to touch someone in the working context conveys superiority. A boss can pat his or her staff on the back, but they probably wouldn't appreciate it if their staff reciprocated. A pat on the back is an authoritative action. When it remains unchallenged, a hierarchy is established.

A good way of putting things back on an even footing is to look for an immediate opportunity to touch them back in a different manner. You might say, 'Excuse me', as you pick a hair off their jacket, or 'You've brushed up against some dust', as you sweep their chest, arm or shoulder briskly with the back of your hand.

The use of gestures

Gestures can either reinforce your communication or they can draw attention away from what you are saying. They should be used prudently, therefore, to maximize their effect.

Gestures include everything from 'windmill' arms (sit on your hands if this is you) to almost imperceptible movements of the face, head, torso or arms – they rarely involve the use of the legs.

The most common gestures are made with hands alone and they serve to emphasize what is being said by the mouth.

The type of gesture you choose to use can indicate something about your personality. If you 'prod the air' more than artistically necessary, you will appear aggressive. Open gestures, arms out away from the body, can indicate an open and warm personality. Be too energetic and untidy with your movements and you will come across as shambolic and disorganized. This is especially true if the style of your dress also tends to be untidy or too casual.

TIP *Assertive gestures tend towards the moderate ground. Timing and relevance are crucial. They should flow smoothly and mirror as closely as possible what is being said.*

Developing rapport

Empathizing with another does not depend solely on the words you use. Much of the rapport is carried in your body language.

If you watch two people talking enthusiastically and unselfconsciously, you will probably notice that their bodies take on virtually the same demeanour. For example, both may have crossed their legs, put an elbow on the table and their chin in the palm of their hands. If they are drinking, you will often find that the drinks diminish at exactly the same rate. They will have *matched* and *mirrored* each other's behaviour. If you do this consciously, but subtly, you will find that your ability to build rapport will have improved greatly.

Should you find yourself in an unpleasant or fraught conversation and you wish to alleviate the tension, it is possible to do this also by matching and mirroring the other's body language. Having matched and held their body position for some time, you can start moving your own body towards a more relaxed position. You will soon find that they start mirroring you and the tension will fade. It is impossible to remain aggressive when you are physically relaxed.

> **TIP**
>
> *Beware: if you are not sufficiently subtle in your mirroring and matching skills, it will look as if you are mimicking the other's behaviour. If this is the impression you create, it will be very difficult to make amends.*

Couple this technique with good eye contact, active listening skills, affirming head nods, 'Ah-has', 'Mmms' and so on, and you will be able to build rapport with the best of them.

Being able to empathize with someone involves understanding their feelings by getting beneath the surface. This can often be achieved by being able to relate what they are saying to a similar experience of your own. If you are at sea, however, with no common understanding, the mirroring and matching technique can be used to engender the same feelings in you that are being experienced by the other person. If the other person has lost confidence, for instance, and takes on the foetal position, try it out for yourself and see what emotions it brings up. You will probably gain a better understanding of their feelings and be able to empathize more effectively.

The use of verbal language

The words we choose and the way we construct sentences can assist us in the process of building rapport.

To illustrate this, think of the way we talk to children. We are constantly reflecting back to them the words they use themselves. It has to be said that sometimes we diminish their intellects, but nonetheless the principle is the same. Listen out for the kind of words used by the person with whom you are trying to build rapport and reflect this style of language back to them.

A manager often uses a distinctive language that is related to the function or specialism of his or her role. Finance, information technology, manufacturing, design and development all have their own language. If you use this language back to these specialists, they will feel comfortable with your style. Use a different language, and they will feel alienated.

Here are some examples of language compatibility:

- A **financier's** language includes words like: balance, bottom line, assets, investments, credit, etc.
- Some of the following words would be used by an **information technologist**: logical, image, capacity, network, hardware, upgrade, etc.

The same sentence can be constructed differently for each audience:

- To the **financier**: 'On *balance*, I feel it would be to our *credit*...'
- To the **information technologist**: 'It would seem the most *logical* approach to *upgrade* our *image* by...'

And to a **visionary designer** whose language may include words like see, impact, style, colour, create, proportion, impression, etc., say 'I can *see* that we could *create* the best *impression* by...'

Interpreting body language

BEWARE: this is not an exact science.

When watching someone for the tell-tale signs of a hidden message, don't engage only your brain; engage your senses, too. People often think that they are privy to the inner secrets of another person, but you have to be bordering on the telepathic to know, really.

However, here are a few guidelines to interpreting body language:

- **Be aware of the environment** in which you are making your observation. If it is cold, your subject may have a tense jaw or their arms may be folded tightly across their bodies. In these circumstances, they *may not* be either nervous or aggressive – but then again, *they may*.
- **Watch for 'leakage'.** One example of leakage is someone who is controlling their nerves extremely well, but subconsciously lets them escape through toes curling and uncurling at the end of their shoes; muscles clenching and unclenching round their jaw, grinding teeth, rattling change

in their pocket and quivering knees. As resourceful human beings, we have many such outlets.

- Mostly, look for **discontinuity** and **coincidence.** If someone is pledging their unequivocal support but shaking their head as they do so – watch your back. If someone says 'I never lie' at the same time as moving their pointing finger from side to side – withhold belief in them for a while and watch them closely. This can be a gesture of denial. If someone says, 'I am not interested in scoring points with the boss' and yet is coincidentally around the boss at the most politically charged moments, watch you don't get sideswiped.

- **Watch people's eyes** – it sounds obvious to say that people look where their interest lies, but sometimes, during an unguarded moment, it is interesting to note exactly where this is – or who it is.

- Sometimes it is easier to **identify 'anti' body language** – people tend to be very clear when they dislike someone. You can see it in their eyes and in the way they orientate their bodies away from the object of their distaste. This is the opposite of mirroring. Sometimes their complete and habitual removal from the scene gives the game away.

When people like each other, they get into close proximity – into that personal body space that is circumscribed by 'the egg'. They may touch, they often have good and prolonged eye contact, and they smile, reinforce and reflect each other's behaviour. Sometimes you are aware of 'chemistry', when there are no identifiable body signals. It is interesting to observe this behaviour and speculate on what it is that causes this effect.

Summary

Today we have briefly looked at a very powerful aid to communication – and the interpretation of communication. We have learned that the body will not lie for you. If there is any incongruence between your message and your intention, it will find its way to the surface through 'leakage'. This makes your (and others') motivation visible, much more visible than you probably realized.

Your body, including your eyes and voice – not words – carries about 90 per cent of any message you are trying to convey. Because the proportion is so large, this aspect of communication has powerful potential. If you use your non-verbal knowledge skilfully, you will find that your level of control increases significantly. Beware, however, that you don't treat this aspect of communication as if it were a definitive code. You need to remember to put in it into context so that any risk of misinterpretation is minimized. Also, be aware that you may be looking for confirmation of a story or fantasy you hold about someone. This will result in you force-fitting the outcome of your analysis into a premeditated conclusion, which will 'muddy the water' of your communications.

However, you should now be more aware and be able to body-watch from a more informed position.

Enjoy body-watching!

SUNDAY
MONDAY
TUESDAY
WEDNESDAY
THURSDAY
FRIDAY
SATURDAY

Fact-check (answers at the back)

Think about the following questions and use them to develop your body language.

1. Body language is a powerful channel for communication. Which of the following statements is true?
a) Communicating without the visual channel (without seeing the communicator's body) can be more revealing ❏
b) By definition, gestures are distracting and misleading ❏
c) Most of the message is contained by the words used ❏
d) Tone, pitch and volume of the voice are considered to be part of body language ❏

2. When someone in the work context pats you on the back to establish their seniority, what can you do to redress the balance?
a) Shrug their hand away and tell them you don't appreciate their touch ❏
b) Pat them back immediately in like manner ❏
c) Find an opportunity to make physical contact in a different, but appropriate way ❏
d) Stand on a chair to make them feel small! ❏

3. What are gestures useful for achieving?
a) Drawing attention to yourself ❏
b) Maximizing the drama of your message ❏
c) Emphasizing what you are saying ❏
d) Distracting people from what you're actually saying! ❏

4. Empathizing with another is very helpful in building rapport. What can you do to establish an initial connection with someone?
a) Tell them what you think they should feel ❏
b) Mirror and match their body language ❏
c) Share your story with them, assuming that your experience will match theirs ❏
d) Say: 'I know how you feel!' ❏

5. Most people use their own distinctive language in their communications. If you want to establish rapport, what can you do to make a connection with them?
a) Use your own distinctive language to draw their attention to your message ❏
b) Reflect back language similar to their own ❏
c) Say you don't understand what they're saying and ask them to speak in English ❏
d) Get out a dictionary and make a play of looking up their words ❏

6. Body language can be used to assist in the interpretation of someone's message. What is the secret of body language?
a) It is an exact science and the code is well known ❏
b) It points towards what's going on under the surface ❏
c) It enables you to cover up what you're really saying ❏
d) It enables you to tell when someone's lying! ❏

7. In terms of body language, what is leakage?
a) The secretion of unpleasant bodily fluids ❏
b) The release of stress in repetitive small movements ❏
c) Spitting and spluttering during speech ❏
d) Excusing oneself repeatedly to go to the bathroom ❏

8. What techniques can you use on the telephone to convey the signals that your body would send if you were face to face?
a) Make exaggerated gestures to compensate for not being in front of each other ❏
b) Signpost what's going on for you – 'I was quiet because I was distracted momentarily.' ❏
c) Talk more loudly ❏
d) Make use of your invisibility to sit with your feet on the desk ❏

9. What do you notice when two people are locked in great conversation?
a) They both talk at the same time ❏
b) They mirror and match each other ❏
c) They each agree with everything the other person says ❏
d) They finish each other's sentences ❏

10. Tall people have an advantage because...
a) People are frightened of them ❏
b) They take up lots of space and have natural impact ❏
c) They can see over everyone's heads ❏
d) They can walk faster than anyone else ❏

SUNDAY
MONDAY
TUESDAY
WEDNESDAY
THURSDAY
FRIDAY
SATURDAY

SATURDAY

Personal
power

We have almost come full circle now, so to close this week's learning, we will discuss personal power – how to win it, how to hold on to it and how to succeed with it.

In the sense that we're using it, personal power is correlated with confidence and goal clarity. It's about believing in what you want and going out to get it. For those who are not naturally blessed with personal power, it is a quality that is worth striving for, and it does take some striving to acquire it. However, with consciousness and dedication, this prize can be won and used to enhance our lives and successes.

The interesting thing about personal power is that you don't have to be born particularly advantaged to have it. It is not dependent upon your looks, size, intelligence, wealth or talents. Some of these may help; but the good news is, anyone can acquire personal power.

Most, or all, of the following qualities are found in powerful people:

- clarity of vision
- well-defined values and beliefs
- confidence
- powerful communication
- an ability to build relationships.

Power remains only with those who respect it. There may be a short-term gain for those who win power through confidence tricks, but it is inevitable that their fall from power will be in direct proportion to the 'con'.

Let's take each element of personal power and examine it separately.

Clarity of vision

It is essential to create a framework upon which you can hang your power. It is only when you know where you are going and are 100-per-cent committed to getting there that you can plan the way forward to your success. It doesn't matter which path you take, or whether you change the route from time to time, as long as you keep your eye on the goal.

Identifying the goal in the first place does require vision. Once you have this, and this is usually acquired through self-knowledge, the rest will fall into place.

If you have difficulty establishing your primary goal, start with a series of smaller ones. These will soon form a pattern that will lead you towards an understanding of what you wish to achieve. Ask yourself where you would like to be in 10, 20 or 50 years' time. Is maintaining your present course and direction sufficient to give you long-term satisfaction? Don't be concerned if your goal is extraordinarily ambitious. All those who have succeeded started out with 'impossible dreams'. Equally, don't be ashamed if your goal is not particularly ambitious. This means that you are meeting your own needs extremely well and puts you way ahead of the game.

Visionaries take the following steps to create a framework upon which they can build their successes. They...

- identify personal goals
- see their goals clearly and imagine what it is like to have reached them

- make a commitment to achieve them by a certain time
- act as if their goals have already been achieved.

If you don't put a time limit on the attainment of your goals, your mind will always think of them as being in the future. Acting as if you have already reached your goals will help to bring them into the present.

Test out these steps for yourself. Start small to gain confidence in the process.

Well-defined values and beliefs

Know what you value and believe. This is really much more difficult than it appears because values and beliefs may change over time, especially if your circumstances change dramatically for one reason or another. Dig deep, though; these underpin all your behaviours.

In the process of getting to know your values and beliefs you will have to ask yourself certain questions. For example, what price are you prepared to pay for your success...

- **personally?** – intimate relationships (partner, family, friends)
- **ethically?** – what you feel is right or wrong; what you need to do to feel good about yourself
- **professionally?** – career progression, promotion
- **politically?** – being in the right place at the right time.

If you ask a successful person the question 'What price are you prepared to pay for your success?', they will often have a clear, well-thought-out answer that is right for them. They are absolutely comfortable living within the framework of their values and beliefs. Any conflict – and conflict will develop from time to time as the balance of their life changes – will be addressed in the light of this value set.

Confidence

Here, we get back to the basics of **successful assertiveness.** Respect and honour yourself. You are as worthy as the next person.

Self-worth is the precursor to building confidence. If you believe in yourself, others will, too.

True confidence enables you to handle any situation well. Even in situations that you have not met before, you will be able to draw on your experience and extrapolate from your past behaviour to meet the needs of the moment.

A sudden lack of confidence can petrify and paralyse the mind and all coping mechanisms disappear. This rapid evacuation of all that you have learned will undermine your attempts at building confidence and put you back to square one again. So be kind to yourself; know that these things happen to everybody and that you are still a worthy individual. Forgive what you perceive to be your mistakes and move on.

The more you practise assertive behaviour, the less often sudden losses in confidence will happen. As with your goals (gaining confidence may be one of them, of course), try believing that you have already succeeded and act that way. It will soon become a reality.

Powerful communication

Powerful people are often extremely good communicators. Their communication skills are characterized by typical assertive behaviour.

Having a vision is not enough. The only way a vision becomes a reality is through motivating others to play their part, and the only way to motivate is to communicate. Only in very rare cases are visions actualized in a vacuum; usually they are dependent upon someone, or many people, co-operating in some way.

Not many of us are natural orators but we can learn from those who are. Here are a few qualities that you can learn to develop in yourself.

- **vision** (remember Martin Luther King's 'I have a dream...' speech)
- **belief** – in your purpose, your own ability and the ability of your team
- **acute observation** (listening, watching, sensing)
- ability to develop **empathy**
- ability to judge the **mood of the moment** and respond appropriately (flexibility/intuition)
- a sense of **timing** and **theatre**.

Powerful communicators regard their public appearances as theatrical performances. They create an impact, build tension, move their audience and leave them on a 'high'.

An ability to build relationships

It is often difficult to build and maintain relationships at the best of times, but it is especially difficult when driven by the work environment. Nonetheless, this ability is crucial if you wish to rise to the top.

There is no magic formula for developing good relationships and they can be stamped with a variety of styles – friendly, nurturing, respectful, mysterious, controlling, aggressive and so on. Try to identify your own style and check out the impression you create with colleagues.

Professional relationships can be troublesome because they have to be developed with people who are imposed upon us, not chosen by us. Indeed, we might actively avoid some of our colleagues when out of the work environment. Building good relationships therefore demands patience, determination and the ability to step back and see things from a different perspective.

Most people do not try to be bad or difficult. If this is the behaviour that they exhibit, it usually indicates that they hold a belief that is being challenged. If you encounter this behaviour as a manager, you may need to spend some time delving below the surface to understand the problem. Beware, however; you cannot merely go through the motions, and you may learn some unpalatable truths about yourself in the process.

Much can be done to maintain relationships remotely (by telephone, letter, email, etc.) but first you have to know and understand the people who work around you. This is done usefully at times when the pressure is off or at times when you socialize together. There is a fine line to tread between being too involved and too remote. You will have to determine the best balance for yourself; but remember that power holders are often characterized by a certain amount of mystique.

Summary

Today we have briefly touched upon the dominant features of personal power. You may want to seek feedback on how you come across. Sometimes we make the mistake of believing that others hold the same belief about us as we do ourselves – either positively or negatively. We may think that they don't see our lack of personal power because we spend time hiding it. Or we may think that they interpret our over-domineering style as powerful. It is worth getting feedback from a trusted source so that you know where your starting point is. It may be painful (or it may not!) but having clarity in terms of how you are seen is really valuable.

SUNDAY

MONDAY

TUESDAY

WEDNESDAY

THURSDAY

FRIDAY

SATURDAY

End-of-week summary

Wherever you're starting from, having picked your way through the week's lessons, you should now have the basic tools to move forward as a successful and assertive professional.

Successful assertiveness ultimately boils down to three main points:

1 Understand yourself (values, beliefs, the whys and wherefores of your nature).
2 Know yourself (wants, predispositions, ambitions, desires).
3 Value yourself (confidence, rights).

From this position of knowledge, you will be well placed to make your own choices – about how you wish to be perceived, how to plan your career and how to create and manage your impression.

Good luck, and enjoy being assertive!

Fact-check (answers at the back)

Think about the following questions and use them to develop your personal power.

1. What is personal power?
a) It is 'Popeye' physical strength ❑
b) It is the confidence to know what you want and know what you need to do to get it ❑
c) It is the ability to dominate situations ❑
d) It is the ability to delegate ❑

2. What do people with personal power possess? Identify the odd one out!
a) Clarity of vision ❑
b) Values and beliefs ❑
c) A position high up in the hierarchy of an organization ❑
d) Ability to build rapport ❑

3. We are goal-oriented beings. What is your goal for the future?
a) 1–5 years from now ❑
b) 5–10 years from now ❑
c) Lifetime goal ❑
d) I don't have a goal ❑

4. Which of these statements about goals is true?
a) Goals get in the way of spontaneity ❑
b) Goals are pointless because they always change with circumstances ❑
c) Goals help us make relevant decisions and take appropriate action ❑
d) Goals are always out of reach ❑

5. How easy do you find it to articulate your vision?
a) I carry a clear vision for myself and can describe it easily ❑
b) I have a vision but it changes so regularly that I don't bother to talk about it ❑
c) People tend to laugh at my vision when I talk about it, thinking it's too fanciful ❑
d) Because I can't control events, I don't have a vision ❑

6. If your relationship building style were assertive, what should it look like?
a) Friendly yet firm ❑
b) Political and manipulative ❑
c) Wilful and commanding ❑
d) Easily biddable ❑

7. If you are engaged in a 'challenging' relationship, what assumption may help you get it back on track again?
a) They may feel misunderstood and unfairly judged ❑
b) They may be disruptive and difficult ❑
c) They may hold a grudge against you for no good reason ❑
d) They may be trying to make you look bad ❑

8. What feedback have you had about your personal power quotient?

a) I'm often told I'm too aggressive ❏

b) I don't receive feedback – and I don't ask for it! ❏

c) I seem to enjoy healthy, co-operative and productive relationships and people tell me they enjoy working with me ❏

d) People say that I'll never get anywhere being as quiet as a mouse! ❏

9. If you had to deal with a conflict in your team, how would you do so assertively?

a) I'd tell the opposing parties to get a life and sort it out! ❏

b) I'd encourage each party to listen to each other's point of view and find some common ground ❏

c) I'd try to resolve the issue for them ❏

d) I wouldn't get involved at all. It's not my business ❏

10. How satisfied are you with your assertiveness skills?

a) I am assertive in my dealings with others and feel comfortable with this ❏

b) I am assertive sometimes but need to practise more in 'difficult' situations ❏

c) I am not particularly assertive but would like to be ❏

d) I get hyped up and tend to dominate situations ❏

7 × 7

Seven key ideas

1 Assertiveness is a choice. It's not something that you have to do all the time!
2 Assertive communication is a win/win style of ommunication. It allows both parties to feel heard and acknowledged.
3 Being assertive is contingent upon you knowing what you want to communicate and communicating it consistently.
4 Finding and flexing an assertive communication style is the beginning of self-understanding.
5 Sometimes being passive, or being aggressive, is assertive (inasmuch as you are choosing to communicate in the most effective way for a particular situation).
6 Listening is a major part of being assertive. Indeed, the balance of listening to speaking should be, at the very least, 2:1 – if not 5:1!
7 Assertive communication also allows you to raise your children and manage your pets effectively.

Seven best resources

1 http://www.mindtools.com/pages/article/Assertiveness.htm –Assertiveness: Working WITH People, Not Against Them (Management Training and Leadership Training, Online)
2 http://www.wikihow.com/Be-Assertive – How to Be Assertive
3 *Assertiveness Pocketbook* by Max A. Eggert – full of good advice on how to overcome self-defeating beliefs, and deal with common problem areas
4 *Brilliant Assertiveness: What the most assertive people know, do and say* by Dannie Lu Carr – practical and accessible, *Brilliant Assertiveness* examines what it means to be assertive and contains exercises and case studies to help you establish your assertiveness skills.

5 iTunes app: *Confidence Booster: Self-Esteem and Assertiveness Training* by Sean Gohara – a walk-through guide on boosting self-esteem and assertiveness utilizing powerful techniques to take you through a full 'internal transformation'

6 *How to Say 'No': Politely but firmly take back control of your time and your life* by Claire Shannon – if you find yourself trying to please everyone but, in doing so, fail to please yourself, this is for you!

7 *Emotional Intelligence: 21 ultimate tips for gaining control over your emotions and becoming a boss of your thoughts and behaviour* by Joseph Sanchez

Seven things to avoid

1 Try not to confuse aggression (you win, they lose) with assertiveness (you win, they win). Assertiveness does not always mean that you get your own way!

2 Don't try to be assertive ALL the time! It can become a tyranny if you beat yourself up every time assertiveness eludes you – and you can become a 'communication tyrant' to others!

3 Try not to expect everyone to have the same communication style as you. By listening and asking questions, you can help others express themselves more effectively.

4 Beware of responding to emails emotionally and instinctively. Put them to one side while you think about what you want to say and how you're going to say it.

5 Don't try to assert yourself at every opportunity. Sometimes, it's best to take yourself off duty and let things go. Ask yourself, 'Will my intervention make a positive difference?'

6 Try not to criticize or judge others' approach to their communication. Remember what it was like when you were not consistently assertive and be generous to those who are trying!

7 Expecting yourself to get it 'right' all the time. With the best will in the world, you're likely to find yourself falling back into your old habits from time to time. Just review what happened and try again!

Seven inspiring people

1 Paloma Faith – a songwriter, singer and all-round performer. Paloma is distinctively herself, with no compromises. Yet she engages empathically with her art and those that surround her. A marvellous role model of international standing.
2 HRH Prince Harry – another uncompromisingly authentic human being with a big heart for doing important work and having a great time. He is lovely to his grandmother, too!
3 Angela Merkel, Chancellor of Germany – conducts herself with great authority, consistency and genuineness in a tough political context as a minority representative of women.
4 Dame Judi Dench – a brilliant and acclaimed actress who brings her personality fully to her audiences. She has endured serious personal loss yet acts as an exemplar of dignity, courage... and humour.
5 Malala Yousafzai – a fabulously brave young Pakistani woman who defied the Taliban, after being shot, by advocating education for girls. At age 17, she became the youngest ever recipient of a Nobel Prize.
6 David Beckham – formerly a footballer with Manchester United, he played for a number of clubs in Europe and America while also being the captain of the England team. He has been a Goodwill Ambassador for UNICEF since his early football career. A good father and a good role model.
7 Sir David Attenborough – primarily known as a naturalist and broadcaster, he has travelled to the most remote parts of the world to bring unique images of animals and descriptions of their lives to television audiences. The enduring image of him being the plaything of two baby gorillas in Rwanda is perhaps defining!

Seven great quotes

1 'The difference between successful people and really successful people is that really successful people say no to almost everything.' Warren Buffett
2 'It's never too late to be what you might have been.' George Eliot
3 'If liberty means anything at all, it means the right to tell people what they don't want to hear.' George Orwell
4 'Get up, stand up / Stand up for your rights. / Get up, stand up, / Don't give up the fight.' Bob Marley
5 'Your playing small does not serve the world. There is nothing enlightened about shrinking so that other people won't feel insecure around you. We are all meant to shine.' Marianne Williamson.
6 'Be yourself; everyone else is already taken.' Oscar Wilde
7 'You may not control all the events that happen to you, but you can decide not to be reduced by them.' Maya Angelou

Seven things to do today

1 Decide how you want to communicate and give yourself some early targets to achieve to get you going.
2 Listen to yourself in communication with others and see whether you can identify your dominant communication style.
3 Identify a role model, observe them in dialogue and see what they do that you could also do – authentically.
4 Pick up a few sentences that allow you to open a 'difficult' conversation assertively.
5 Read through your written communications and try to view them from the other person's perspective. Try to imagine the impression that they'll get from them.
6 Tackle a difficult conversation that you've been putting off for a while.

7 Ask a trusted friend to hear you rehearse some 'openers' or anticipated responses and give you feedback. Once you've heard yourself saying things differently (and to your satisfaction), you'll begin to find your new style more easily accessible and familiar.

Seven trends for tomorrow

1 With the increase of social media in all aspects of life (including the professional), think about how your communication style is conveyed in the 'sound bites' you choose. Without much context, meaning can easily be distorted.

2 People tend to be accessible, online, all the time. This creates a willingness in them to interrupt face-to-face communication in order to respond to a ring or a bleep – or a theme tune! 'Instantaneousness' is the biggest disturbance in the communication field and can lead less assertive people to feel unimportant and uninteresting.

3 Virtual working patterns are both a blessing and a curse for the unassertive communicator. They are a blessing inasmuch as there is often more time available to plan responses to questions or prompts. They are a curse inasmuch as messages are devoid of the physical clues and cues that allow appropriate responses to be given and it is easy to misunderstand and miscommunicate messages.

4 The increase in multigenerational working environments means that different styles of communication are called for and different meanings are projected on to different communication styles. It seems that we must be multi-skilled and multi-talented in order to 'hold true to ourselves'.

5 Globalization brings with it the need to communicate across multi-variant cultures and social divides. Being assertive in one cultural context may be received as aggressive in

another. It is important to take some time to understand the social mores of those with whom you are communicating.

6 Virtual, yet face-to-face, meeting options are increasing in popularity due to the cost benefit. This type of meeting requires a particular type of etiquette to compensate for the physical distance and atmospheric difference. To avoid confusion or mixed messages, communicators must be participative and their communication clear and unambiguous.

7 A 'counter-trend' may emerge that addresses the issue of privacy and confidentiality. To avoid old photographs and 'sensitive' conversations from getting into the hands of those with few reasons to respect their provenance, people may go back to hushed conversations and contact prints!

Answers

Sunday: *Individual responses*

Monday: 1a; 2c; 3d; 4c; 5c; 6c; 7c; 8a; 9d; 10d

Tuesday: 1d; 2d; 3d; 4d; 5d; 6c; 7b; 8c; 9c; 10c

Wednesday: 1b, 2d; 3c; 4c; 5c; 6c; 7c; 8b; 9c; 10d

Thursday: 1d; 2d; 3c; 4d; 5d; 6b; 7c; 8d; 9d; 10d

Friday: 1d; 2c; 3c; 4b; 5b; 6b; 7b; 8b; 9b; 10b

Saturday: 1b; 2c; 3 *individual response*; 4c; 5 *individual response*; 6a; 7a; 8 *individual response*; 9b; 10 *individual response*

ALSO AVAILABLE IN THE 'IN A WEEK' SERIES

For information about other titles in the 'In A Week' series, please visit
www.teachyourself.co.uk

MORE TITLES AVAILABLE IN THE 'IN A WEEK' SERIES

For information about other titles in the 'In A Week' series, please visit
www.teachyourself.co.uk

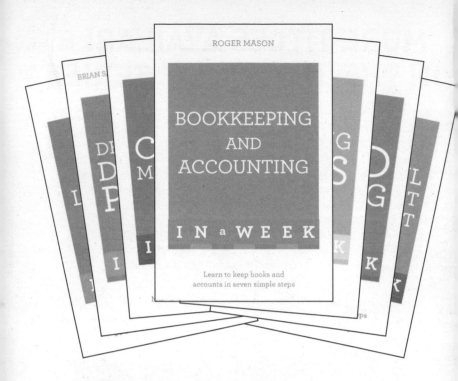

YOUR FASTEST ROUTE TO SUCCESS

LEARN IN A WEEK WHAT THE EXPERTS LEARN IN A LIFETIME

For information about other titles in the 'In A Week' series, please visit www.teachyourself.co.uk